LIVING UNBREAKABLE

The No-BS Playbook for Reinventing Yourself

Jessica Spence

❀ LUCKY BOOK PUBLISHING

If you're holding this book, chances are something inside you is ready to rise.

The Phoenix on the cover isn't just a design choice; it's a declaration. This mythical bird is known for bursting into flames, crumbling into ashes, and then being reborn more powerful than ever before.

Sound familiar?

It's the story of every woman who's ever hit rock bottom, questioned everything, and still chosen to rebuild, piece by piece, breath by breath, sometimes in tears and sometimes in total badass mode. It's the story of reinvention, resilience, and the kind of strength that's forged in fire.

This book is my ashes-to-alchemy story. And maybe, just maybe, it's a mirror for yours too.
So, before we dive in, know this: Rock bottom isn't the end, it's the spark.

And the Phoenix? She's you.

Dedication

To my little girls:

I know that the universe brought us together to break cycles, live with bravery, and be the light. My hope is that one day, you'll grow up knowing that you are bold, resilient beings who lead with love, kindness, and unwavering strength.

You are my everything. Shine Bright my little diamonds.

To Brad, my soulmate:

You choose me and the girls every single day, loving us with a depth that knows no bounds. You've embraced them as your own, showering them with the same unwavering love and care you give me. Through your presence, you've gently guided me back into my feminine power, reminding me what it means to be loved fully and deeply. Your belief in us is endless, and your love is the anchor that holds our family together.

You fill our lives with adventure, laughter, and light, whether you're teaching the girls to ride bikes or swim like little fish, or taking us on "adventures" (that we may not have fully signed up for, ahem, mountain biking). Somehow, you make even the wildest detours fun.

Thank you for being the earth angel who keeps us grounded while also convincing us we can fly, sometimes literally. I am forever grateful.

MY GIFT TO YOU

I am so glad you're here!

As my Gift to you, get FREE Access to the Living Unbreakable bonus content by scanning the QR Code below or visiting NextStepMortgageGroup.com/book

My Dream

My dream for this book is deeply personal and ever-evolving. I wrote it for the woman who's questioning everything she was taught to be. For the mother trying to hold it all together while secretly falling apart. For the high-achiever who feels like she's drowning behind the scenes. For the ones who smile on the outside but are silently screaming for more.

I wrote it for you, and for every version of me I've had to become, un-become, and rebuild along the way.

The world doesn't make space for women to unravel without judgment. We're expected to juggle, succeed, raise babies, bounce back, and stay grateful through it all. But the truth? Reinvention is messy. And necessary. And beautiful.

This book isn't about having all the answers; it's about giving you permission to stop pretending you do. It's a no-BS playbook for coming home to yourself. For unlearning the rules that were never meant for you. For rising stronger, softer, louder, and more you than ever before.

I hope the words in these pages meet you where you are, in your stuckness, your soul shift, your chaos, or your clarity. And I hope they remind you that what you're moving through is not a setback—it's a starting point.

Whether you're reading this with tears in your eyes, a fire in your belly, or hope in your heart, I'm right here with you.

My dream is that when you close this book, you feel seen, empowered, and utterly unbreakable.

Let's walk this journey together.

And if this message speaks to you, let's connect beyond the pages.

I'd be honored to speak on your podcast, show up for your book club, or join your panel or event to keep this conversation going.

Add me on Instagram @jessica_spence88, tag your favorite quote, or just slide into my DMs and say hi. I'd love to hear your story, too.

We rise louder when we rise together.

Jessica

Author, Mama, Reinvention Queen, and your loudest cheerleader.

TABLE OF CONTENTS

"Healing is the new glow up.

Kindness is the new status symbol.

And self-awareness?
That's the new sexy.

You want to change the world?

Start with the mirror."

– Jessica Spence

PROLOGUE

It was 4 months postpartum. I had 60 extra pounds hanging around like an uninvited guest who refused to leave, my anxiety and panic disorder were running the show, and I was stuck in a toxic marriage. If my life were a movie, it would've been a tragicomedy, one of those indie films where the main character stares out the window a lot while sad music plays.

I could barely leave the house. The world outside felt too overwhelming, too big, too much. So instead, I stayed in my nursery, trapped in the same four walls, breastfeeding my baby while feeling like I was slowly disappearing. On this particular day, the weight of it all became unbearable. I sat there, tears streaming down my face, my mind spiralling, exhausted from fighting the invisible battle inside me.

And in that moment, raw, broken, desperate, I did something I had never done before. I begged.

I looked up at the ceiling, at the universe, at something bigger than me, and I pleaded for a sign. Anything. Some kind of confirmation that I was meant to stay on this earth, even for just one. More. Day.

I waited. Nothing. No divine lightning bolt, no voice from the heavens, not even a suspiciously well-timed song lyric. Just silence.

And then, a knock.

A tiny, soft knock at the door.

"Mama, I need you."

It was my 3-year-old.

At first, I thought I imagined it. But there she was, on the other side of the door, needing me. And in that split second, the fog in my brain parted just enough for one piercing thought to break through:

She needs me. They need me.

And then, the one that changed everything:

I need me.

For the first time in forever, I realized that I wasn't just existing for my kids, I had to exist for me. I had spent years drowning in anxiety, in self-doubt, in a life that wasn't aligned with who I truly was. But no one was coming to save me. No flashing sign, no guardian angel with a to-do list. I was the one who had to get up, one day at a time, and choose myself.

It wasn't a grand, cinematic moment of enlightenment. It was small. Simple. But it was mine. And it was enough to make me get up, wipe my tears (with a side of baby vomit), and take the first step toward the life I knew I was meant to live.

This was the day everything changed. And this book? Think of it as my No-BS Survival Guide, equal parts love letter, pep talk, and tough-love nudge, sprinkled with just enough chaos to keep it interesting.

Trust me, you're gonna want to stick around.

Xo J

INTRODUCTION

Buckle Up! It's Time to Meet Your Unbreakable Self

Just between us, life has thrown me into the deep end more times than I can count. As a military brat, I became an expert at packing up my life, waving goodbye to friends, and learning to adapt to new places before I even knew what "stability" was. You'd think all that moving would've made me fearless. Nope. It mostly made me a pro at pretending I had my life together when, in reality, I was just trying to figure out where I belonged.

Fast forward a bit, and I found myself battling a whole different kind of challenge, one that couldn't be solved by a new zip code. I carried the weight (literally) of obesity, along with anxiety, panic attacks, and agoraphobia, which made stepping outside feel like stepping into a battlefield. And just when I thought life had maxed out on plot twists, I found myself walking away from a toxic marriage with my two little girls, a handful of belongings, and zero clue how I was going to rebuild.

But here's the thing about hitting rock bottom, you get a front-row seat to the kind of growth that only happens when you have no choice but to rise. That's when everything shifted. I let go of the life that was breaking me and stepped into the one I was meant to create.

I reconnected with Brad, my soulmate, my anchor, my unexpected happily-ever-after. He not only loved me fiercely, but he also loved my daughters as his own. He reminded me what it meant to feel safe, cherished, and, dare I say it, taken on spontaneous adventures like we were in a rom-com.

As I began to heal through the process, so did everything else. I lost 60 pounds, not just from my body but from my soul. I became obsessed (okay, deeply passionate) about health, wellness, spirituality, and personal growth. I devoured everything I could on holistic healing, energy alignment, and becoming the kind of person who doesn't just survive adversity but thrives through it.

Now, here's where you come in. This book isn't just about my wild ride, it's about you. It's about the fire inside you that's been waiting to be unleashed. It's about recognizing that every setback, every challenge, and every "WTF is happening?!" moment is actually shaping you into the strongest, boldest version of yourself.

I hope as you turn these pages, you feel a spark, maybe even a full-blown wildfire, of inspiration to take control of your story. Because no matter where you are right now, one thing is certain: You have everything you need to transform your life. And trust me, it's going to be one hell of a journey.

So, here's the deal, at the end of every chapter, you'll find a No-BS Reinvention Reflection. These aren't just cute journal prompts or feel-good quotes, they're the same gritty, honest reflections I used (and still use) as I fought my way through the mess, the magic, and the miracles of reinventing myself.

I won't pretend it's always pretty. It's not. Some of it might sting a little, some of it might crack you wide open, but all of it will make you stronger. And the best part? I'm not handing you advice from some mountaintop; I'm right here, in the trenches with you, figuring it out too.

This isn't just an average self help tool, it's The No-BS Playbook to Reinventing Yourself. And you, my friend, are about to become completely, unapologetically, unbreakable.

Let's go.

PART ONE: The Breaking Point

Chapter 1
Blame Game? Nah,
Let's Play 'Own Your Stuff' Instead

There's nothing like a personal apocalypse to wake you up.

I remember sitting in that nursery glider, the one that squeaked every time I rocked back and forth, like it was mocking me. I was exhausted, emotionally tapped out, smelling like breastmilk and dry shampoo, silently wondering how the hell I got here.

She needs me. They need me. I need me, I repeated to myself.

And then, because the universe has a twisted sense of humor, I picked up my phone to scroll... and there she was.

Some random girl from Instagram, living her best life. You know the one, flawless skin, glowing like she bathes in unicorn tears. Traveling, laughing, working out, sipping smoothies in cute workout sets, surrounded by friends who looked like they stepped out of a damn

Pinterest board. Oh, and her family? Perfect. Like, magazine-cover perfect.

She was everything I dreamed of being...
and then some.

And me? I couldn't even remember the last time I wore pants without an elastic waistband or made it through 24 hours without crying in the bathroom.

But little did I know, that girl, that random scroll, that seemingly insignificant 30-second story?

It was about to change everything.

That night, shortly after the wrath of bedtime snacks came to a close, I slid into her DMs.

Not with confidence. Not with a pitch. Not with a plan.

Just a message from a woman on the edge, whispering through the screen:

"I need something to change. I don't even know what you're doing, but whatever it is... I want in."

She didn't hesitate. She didn't ask for credentials or experience.

She just saw me. And she said, "Welcome to the team."

Her name was Danielle, and to this day, she's one of the most important souls I've ever met.

Because in that moment, when I was drowning in self-doubt, postpartum fog, and a full-blown "what the hell is my life" spiral, she became my lighthouse.

The one who reminded me I wasn't broken, I was just buried.

Buried under guilt. Exhaustion. Mom-mode. Expectations.

And a whole pile of blame that wasn't getting me anywhere.

Danielle didn't save me.

She sparked me.

And that spark?

Was the beginning of my ownership, reinvention, and no-BS personal accountability.

From Spiral to Spark

Danielle had been working with a health and fitness company for years. She had retired herself from dental hygiene, a career I was surviving in, not thriving, and was now building her dream life through digital marketing.

Freedom. Impact. Confidence. A full-body YES to life.

And when she told me there was space to work alongside her, my inner critic practically screamed:

"Excuse me?? You? The mess in stretchy pants with toddler snacks in your hair? You don't even know how to post a story, never mind SELL something!"

I laughed out loud.

Not the cute kind. The "I'm spiraling but hiding it with sarcasm" kind.

Because at the time?

I was 60 pounds overweight.

Anxious. Tired. Isolated.

Emotionally bankrupt and physically drained.

I could barely get myself out the front door without a pep talk, and now I was supposed to convince people to buy a fitness plan?

Why would anyone want to listen to me?

Hell, I didn't even want to listen to me.

But something in me stirred.

Not loudly. Not confidently.

Just a little whisper:

"What if this is the start of your reinvention?"

And that whisper, that tiny voice buried beneath the self-doubt, guilt, and shame?

Was the beginning of a full-body, full-life, full-soul transformation.

The Micro-Moment That Mattered

The next morning, something was different.

I didn't wake up transformed. There were no angels singing. No glow-up montage.

But I woke up with intention, and honestly, that was new for me.

I decided: One small change. Every day. That's it.

So, I dragged myself into the basement, babies crawling all over me like adorable little chaos gremlins.

I had no clue what I was doing. I was literally trying to shove a DVD into some weird cable box-thingy and figure out how to make the grainy workout play on the TV.

It wasn't cute. It wasn't curated. It was chaos.

I tripped over toys.

I couldn't find a clean sports bra that actually fit.

My toddler tried to eat a resistance band.

My dog licked sweat off my leg like she was offering moral support.

But it was a start.

And that alone? Made me smile.

Because for the first time in a long time, I wasn't spiraling.

I wasn't numbing.

I wasn't blaming.

I was doing.

One step.

One squat.

One breath in the opposite direction of where I'd been going.

And that is where the magic begins, not when it's perfect, but when it's yours.

SCIENCE SNAPSHOT 🔋

Small intentional actions, like choosing to move your body or hydrate when you don't feel like it, literally create new neural pathways in the brain. That's neuroplasticity. And every tiny choice? It's shaping your future self.

Cue the Comeback (With Chaos and Coffee)

The truth is, this wasn't my first time trying to "get healthy."

I'd been into health and wellness since I was 21, back when my panic and anxiety disorder first decided to crash the party of my early adulthood.

Back then, I thought I knew what I was doing.

Spoiler alert: I didn't.

It was the golden era of low-fat everything, 1,200-calorie crash diets, and cardio until you cried.

I was out there rollerblading like I was training for the X Games and living on rice cakes like it was a personality trait.

And don't even get me started on the stair climber. I basically climbed Mt. Everest three times a week while blasting early 2000s dance remixes on my iPod Shuffle.

Honestly, I was working so hard to shrink my body... and was still somehow shrinking my joy right along with it.

But hey, at least my calves were fire.

This Time, It Wasn't a "Bounce-Back"...
It Was a Return

Now, standing in my basement, 60 pounds heavier after back-to-back pregnancies, in a body I barely recognized, I realized:

This wasn't about getting "back" to me.

This was about meeting the new me.

The motherhood version. The mature version. The woman who had walked through fire and still showed up.

I wasn't starting from scratch.

I was starting from wisdom.

And damn, did that feel different.

Because here's the kicker: I had already lost 60 pounds after my first pregnancy, three years earlier.

And now?

I was staring down that same mountain again.

But this time, I wasn't doing it with bounce-back optimism and a curated meal plan.

I was doing it with two kids, zero sleep, and a body that felt like it had survived a war.

I was older.

Softer.

Wiser.

And honestly? A little more pissed off.

Because no one talks about the emotional weight of trying to "get back to you" when you don't even know who the hell you is anymore.

But that day, on that cluttered basement floor, with a sippy cup at my feet and a toddler pulling at my leg, I made a decision:

This time would be different.
This wasn't a bounce-back.
This was a breakthrough.

REINVENTION MYTH-BUSTING

"You have to feel confident to start"
No. You just have to be willing.

"Healing has to look aesthetic"
Nah. Most glow-ups start in sweatpants with a messy bun and emotional damage.

"If you're still struggling, you haven't healed"
False. Struggling is often a sign that you're breaking through, not breaking down.

The Real Face of Starting Over

Let's be clear, starting over doesn't look like a polished Instagram carousel or a #motivationmonday reel.

It looks like working out in pajama pants with a baby clinging on tight in her front-facing carrier.

It looks like pressing play on a workout... and then pausing it nine times because someone needs a snack, a wipe, a cry, or your full emotional support.

It looks like restarting. Again.

And again.

And again.

And in that messy, beautiful chaos, something clicked.

For the first time in forever, I wasn't trying to prove anything to anyone.

I wasn't doing it for likes or before-and-after photos.

I was doing it for me.

Accountability Over Aesthetics

Because when I stopped blaming the partner, the pregnancy, the job, the burnout, the timing, or the version of me who "let it all go..."

When I finally got honest about how I'd been abandoning myself?

I took my power back.

And that was the moment I learned the first truth of reinvention:

You can't change your life if you don't own your sh*t.

RESEARCH SNAPSHOT 📷

A 2018 study in The Journal of Positive Psychology found that people who take personal accountability experience greater mental health, increased self-efficacy, and more consistent goal achievement than those who rely on external blame.

You wouldn't stop reading your own story just because you hit a plot twist you didn't like.

The best part of any book or movie is seeing how the main character rises.

So why would you quit on yourself now?

This chapter isn't the ending, it's the setup.

The tension before the breakthrough.

The messy middle before the mic-drop finale.

Remember: you're not just the main character.

You're also the writer, the director, and the one who decides how this story plays out.

So turn the page. The best part is still coming.

No-BS Reinvention Reflection: This is where the transformation begins. No filters. Just truth

1. What excuses have I been clinging to that feel safer than growth?

   _____

   _____

   _____

   _____

2. Where am I blaming others, life, or timing, when deep down, I know it's me avoiding the uncomfortable truth?

   _____

   _____

   _____

   _____

3. Am I ready to own my sh*t, even if that means burning down who I thought I was supposed to be?
   Yes / No / Maybe
   (And what would that look like?)

   _____

   _____

   _____

   _____

Sticky Note for Your Future Self

I don't need a perfect plan. I need
one honest choice. I own my story,
my healing, and my next chapter,
starting now.

Chapter 2
Spoiler Alert, You're Not in Control

Flashback to 2020

I left the marriage. No fanfare. Just two little girls, a few bins, a mama dead set on figuring it out and moved straight into one of my mom's rental properties.

No backup plan. No white picket fence.

Just breast milk, a bunk bed, and a body running on pure adrenaline.

2020 was the official exit out of the only home I ever knew, the memories, the life, the dreams.

But let's rewind for a second, because the plan had been in motion for months.

Late nights in 2019 were spent Googling apartments, crunching budgets, hiding my phone in blankets while I mapped out how the hell I was going to do this.

I wasn't winging it. I was strategizing survival.

My mom, in divine timing, had a rental unit available.

It was a beautiful townhome, fully furnished, clean, safe.

All I needed was a crib for the baby and a bed
for Isabella.

I didn't have much money saved. I was stretched thin.

So my mom bought the girls a bunk bed, the kind of
help I'll never forget.

I packed the basics.

And I left.

No parade. No closure.

Just me, two kids, and a fierce knowing that I wasn't
going back.

Was I scared? Terrified.

But also?

I was free.

I woke up that first morning to silence. Not eggshells.
Not tension.

Just the scent of essential oils, soft light through the
blinds, and Dermot Kennedy playing on Alexa.

It wasn't glamorous. But it was mine.

And I knew, even if I didn't have the full picture, I had
finally taken the first real step.

A few weeks later?

March 13th, 2020.

Pandemic.

Dental office shut down.

Paycheck vanished.

No partner. No clear map.

Just faith.

I had lost people I loved, friends, family, everyone who couldn't accept that I was choosing myself.

I was in full scorched earth mode.

No more shrinking. No more explaining.

If you weren't riding with me, you were getting left behind.

It was the ultimate surrender.

I remember standing in that kitchen, heart pounding, babies asleep upstairs, and whispering:

"Universe, I'm letting go.

I trust you.

Bring me the best.

Show me what I'm made of."

That was the moment I stopped clinging.

And everything began to shift.

Not all at once. Not perfectly.

But finally... honestly.

Spoiler Alert, You're Not In Control

Let me tell you about the time I thought I had my entire life figured out.

We're talking vision boards. Color-coded planners. A five-year roadmap that would make corporate HR weep with pride. My mornings? Aesthetic-level perfection. Lemon water, 10k steps, and affirmations that screamed "abundance mindset."

And then?

Plot. Freaking. Twist.

Life showed up like:

"Aw, sweetie... that's adorable. Anyway, here's a divorce, a global pandemic, custody arrangements that'll break your heart, surprise lawyer fees, an identity crisis, and a full-body emotional meltdown. Enjoy!"

Turns out? I wasn't in control.

I was just really damn good at performing like I was.

But here's where it gets interesting:

One year into my so-called "reinvention," things were actually going well.

I had lost 60 pounds.

I was glowing in a way no filter could fake.

I finally felt like the kind of woman my daughters deserved to watch rise.

I was thriving in my digital marketing business, so much so, I cut back my dental hygiene hours and was home more.

More presence. More purpose. More of me.

I had finally become everything I thought I was working toward.

But reinvention? It doesn't end when your jeans fit again.

It doesn't stop when the world claps for your comeback.

It deepens.

Because just when you think you've made it, that's when the real work begins.

I thought I had reached the mountaintop.

But the truth? That was just basecamp.

Enter: Surrender

Not the curated kind with rose quartz in your bra and a salt lamp glowing in the background.

I'm talking about the real kind.

The raw, unfiltered, fall-apart-on-the-bathroom-floor kind.

The kind of surrender that doesn't come when you're peaceful and enlightened...

It comes when you're exhausted.

When Plan A blew up, Plan B ghosted you, and Plan C involves Googling:

"How to start over at thirty-something while holding it all together."

Surrender doesn't mean you're giving up.

It means you're finally done fighting battles that were never yours to begin with.

> ### PSYCH INSIGHT
>
> When your nervous system is stuck in hypervigilance, it associates control with safety. Letting go doesn't feel good at first, because your brain is wired to equate "doing" with "surviving." But true healing begins the moment your body finally exhales.

It's that moment when white-knuckling life stops looking like strength... and starts feeling like fear.

Surrender is the moment you unclench.

You stop gripping the timeline.

You stop forcing the outcome.

You stop trying to control every detail, because you finally understand:

Control isn't clarity. It's survival mode in disguise.

And when I finally stopped trying to glue my old life back together with hustle and hope?

That's when things started to shift.

Not magically.

Not instantly.

But authentically.

When the Bathroom Floor Becomes Sacred Ground

Surrender isn't sexy.

It doesn't look good on the outside.

But it's sacred.

Because it's in the letting go, of expectations, of perfection, of performing, that you finally make space to meet yourself.

And sometimes?

Surrender looks like sitting on the bathroom floor, trying to catch your breath... while your whole world reorders itself without your permission.

It looks like watching your children, your literal heart walking around outside your body, learn how to navigate life without you being there for every bedtime, every scraped knee, every in-between moment.

It's grieving the version of motherhood you thought you'd always have.

COMPASSION ROOTED UNDERSTANDING 🫶

Grief doesn't only show up in death. It's the body's response to perceived safety being lost: identities, routines, relationships. It whispers, "This isn't how it was supposed to be." And healing begins when we allow ourselves to answer back, "But it's still going to be okay."

It's holding space for the ache of missing them... while still choosing to become someone they'll be proud to come home to.

This is the kind of grief no one warns you about.

The kind that's invisible, but all-consuming.

The kind that whispers, "Are you sure this is worth it?"

And somewhere in your soul, you answer:

Yes.

Because I'm becoming the woman I promised I'd be.

For the little girl I was.

For the daughters I'm raising.

For the cycle I came here to break.

When I was Clinging to Control...	When I Finally Surrendered...
Micromanaged everything	Made aligned decisions, not perfect ones
Was exhausted by expectation	Felt peace in progress
Tolerated disrespect to avoid conflict	Set boundaries and found my power
Looked successful on the outside	Felt free on the inside
Needed approval	Trusted myself

Expectations = Disappointments in Heels

Let's unpack expectations for a second.

Because while surrender is a softening, expectations are often the iron grip that keeps us stuck, choking on old timelines and outdated "shoulds."

Expectations are sneaky.

They show up dressed like ambition.

They say things like:

"By now, I should be married."

"I should have a house."

"I should be further along."

And just like that, we're measuring our entire worth against a checklist we didn't even write.

PSYCHOLOGY-BACKED TRUTH

Expectations often stem from early childhood conditioning, when love, praise, or safety was conditional on how well we performed. As adults, we repeat this pattern with our goals.

But those scripts?

They aren't yours.

They're outdated software running on your next-level hardware.

And when life doesn't follow the plan?

When the marriage ends, the business pivots, the timeline gets blown to hell?

Expectations don't offer comfort.

They offer disappointment in heels.

The kind that looks fabulous, but absolutely wrecks your feet.

The kind that feels like failure, when it's simply just redirection.

Show the Freedom in Letting Go

Letting go doesn't mean you stop caring.

It means you stop clenching.

You stop gripping so hard to the version of life you thought you were supposed to have, and you start getting curious about the version that's trying to unfold.

NERVOUS SYSTEM NOTE 🧠

Curiosity signals the brain that you're shifting from fight-or-flight to safety. Letting go is a biologically healing act, not weakness, but actual rewiring of your fear centers.

Control is exhausting.

Letting go is liberating.

When I stopped obsessing over timelines, milestones, and social media-worthy perfection?

I finally started to breathe.

I showed up messy. I pivoted.

I let go of the version of me who needed everything to look perfect to feel safe.

Letting go didn't make me less ambitious.

It made me more aligned.

VISUAL: This Is What Healing Actually Looks Like

Healing Isn't:

- Aesthetic flat-lays of candles and journals
- Everyone clapping for your growth
- A straight line from pain to power
- Getting closure from the people who hurt you

Healing Is:

- Saying, "I am allowed to outgrow the version of me that kept everyone else comfortable."
- Crying over people you outgrew
- Leaving when it would be easier to stay
- Being misunderstood and doing it anyway
- Choosing your peace over their comfort

Growth will cost you your comfort, your silence, and the people who only liked the wounded version of you.

The Bridge Theory

There's a concept I read once called The Bridge Theory.

Some people are in your life to get you from one version of yourself to the next.

They're not your forever.

They're the in-between.

The sacred chaos between old identity and new evolution.

And the most compassionate thing you can do, for them and for you, is to release them with love.

Because clinging to what was will never allow you to rise into what is.

Letting go of control doesn't just free you from outcomes...

It frees you from identities that were never fully you to begin with.

And sometimes?

The most powerful version of you emerges only after the old one burns to the ground.

> **BODY BASED WISDOM**
>
> Growth often activates disorientation before clarity. Feeling "lost" is a sign your old identity is breaking apart, and your body is recalibrating to a new baseline of safety.

Call Out the Myth of Control

We've been taught that if we can just plan enough, hustle hard enough, achieve all the shiny gold stars, we'll be safe.

Control = safety.

Control = success.

Control = "Everything will be fine if I just white-knuckle it a little harder."

But here's the truth no one wants to admit:

We don't control the timing.

We don't control other people.

We barely control our Wi-Fi connection on a Zoom call.

What do we control?

How we respond when the entire plan goes up in flames.

No-BS Reinvention Reflection: You can't fake flow. The faster you stop clinging, the faster things click.

1. What part of my life am I still trying to control, even though it's clearly not working?

   _____

   _____

   _____

   _____

   _____

2. If I'm being honest... what am I afraid will happen if I let go of control?

   _____

   _____

   _____

   _____

3. What relationships, environments, or beliefs are starting to feel uncomfortable as I grow?

   _____

   _____

   _____

   _____

Let this be your power pivot.

Less gripping. More growing. Less

forcing. More flowing. Less control.

More truth. Less fear. More freedom.

Let go. Then rise.

Chapter 3
Breakdowns Are Sexy (Eventually)

I was in my living room, throwing punches at the air in a virtual boxing program, sweating, swearing, and sobbing through every round.

It wasn't just a workout.

It was a full-body exorcism.

Every jab, every hook, every uppercut was liberating something inside me, anger, heartbreak, power, hope.

That screen wasn't just showing a trainer.

It was holding space for a woman finally choosing herself.

Ugly crying? Check.

Rage journaling? Double check.

Suddenly listening to 4-hour podcasts on healing while simultaneously googling "WTF is shadow work?"

Absolutely.

This wasn't your cute, glow-up era.

This was the breakdown. The big one.

You don't just hit rock bottom and climb out like some inspiration reel.

First, you sit in the rubble. You stare at the pieces. You doubt you'll ever feel whole again.

But something wild happens when everything falls apart: your nervous system starts whispering, "What if this is where you finally rebuild?"

And it turns out... breakdowns are wildly productive, but only in hindsight.

You don't know you're "transforming." You just think you're losing your entire mind.

You feel like a shell of your former self, floating in a body that doesn't recognize her reflection, crying into your smoothie and making emotional Pinterest boards at 1 a.m.

But you're not lost. You're in the hallway.

The in-between. The moment when the old version of you has crumbled, but the new one hasn't fully arrived.

And while it's excruciating?

It's also essential.

Neuroscience shows that during periods of intense emotional transition, your neural pathways literally reorganize, which explains why you feel foggy, forgetful, and wildly unstable.

Translation?

Your brain is under construction. Be kind to her.

I used to forget everything, names, groceries, passwords, even what day it was. One time I sobbed because I couldn't remember the login to my banking app and convinced myself I was actually losing cognitive function.

Yet, I look back only to realize, I wasn't a mess, I was in the middle of a system upgrade.

Know this, your body doesn't know the difference between a breakup and a bear attack. It just knows something once safe is gone, and now it's on high alert.

That's why you can't focus.

That's why you cry at commercials.

That's why laundry feels like climbing Everest.

I was learning how to be by myself for the first time in a decade.

My ex-husband and I had agreed on a one-day-on, one-day-off schedule with the girls.

And because I was still breastfeeding, I pumped and sent milk like some kind of warrior cow goddess.

She was mostly eating solids by then, but it was the comfort feeds and bedtime snuggles that made it all feel so heavy.

So unfamiliar.

So alone.

But looking back?

That season, what felt like the end of the world, actually saved me.

Because the world had stopped, we had the space to ease into this new reality.

No one was working. Everything was slower.

And for that reason, we were able to do one day on, one day off with the kids, instead of jumping straight into a 2-2-3 or week-on, week-off routine like most co-parents do.

It gave me time.

Time to process not having my babies with me 24/7.

Time to learn how to breathe without them in the room.

Time to grieve the life I thought I'd have, while creating space for the one that was unfolding.

I used to think being a "good mom" meant being available 24/7. That my value was in proximity, in how many dinners I made, how many scraped knees I kissed.

But this experience forced me to redefine what presence actually looks like.

Sometimes, presence is eye contact instead of multitasking.

Sometimes, it's saying no so you can show up better tomorrow.

And sometimes? It's trusting that love can stretch across timelines and households, that your kids feel you even in the quiet.

Turns out, love is way more durable than I gave it credit for.

Of course, the guilt still crept in. Every handoff felt like a little heartbreak.

I'd smile and say, "See you tomorrow!" while my insides screamed, "Don't go."

But I learned to rewrite that guilt.

To remind myself that giving my kids a mom who feels whole, not just present, is the greatest gift I could offer.

Letting go for a day doesn't mean I've failed them.

It means I trust our love enough to stretch.

It wasn't just about learning how to be without a partner; it was about learning how to mother differently.

Shared custody is one of those things people nod at sympathetically but never really get unless they've lived it.

Because it's not just a schedule. It's a soul stretch.

It's sitting in your kitchen, staring at two untouched bowls of mac and cheese because you forgot they weren't coming home that night.

It's tears flowing down your face, into your sweater while folding their laundry, knowing they won't be back until tomorrow.

It's overthinking everything: Did I say the right goodbye? Did I hug them long enough? Did they feel safe, seen, loved?

Some nights I'd fall asleep with their little stuffies beside me, like a ritual to soothe the ache of the empty house.

Other nights I'd scroll through old videos just to hear their laughter again.

No book or parenting course prepares you for the grief of not tucking your kids in every single night.

You grieve them while they're still alive, still happy, just not with you.

And yet, as painful as it was, that sacred pause gave me the chance to build a new kind of bond with them.

One that was slower.

More intentional.

More present.

I realized that motherhood doesn't end when they're not physically beside you.

It expands.

It adapts.

It finds new ways to show up, in voice notes, in packed lunches, in handmade notes tucked into backpacks.

Now I see it so clearly.

It all happened in divine timing.

Not to break me, but to build me.

Slowly. Gently. Powerfully.

The whole world shut down.

No dental hygiene (and no, I don't just mean flossing).

No "let's meet for coffee."

Just me, my two girls, my hormones, and a virtual business I wasn't sure I could keep alive when I barely felt alive.

But then... things began to shift.

The sun started coming out.

The weather warmed.

My sister became my lifeline.

She'd show up daily, sometimes just to go for a walk, rollerblade like 12-year-olds, eat rice bowls and kale, and laugh like idiots.

We had no idea what we were doing, but damn, it felt healing.

I stopped searching for answers and just started being.

Being present.

Being messy.

Being human.

Slowly, the anxiety began to ease. Not because life was magically perfect, but because I started doing the tiniest things that told my body I was safe.

Drinking cold water. Lying on the ground. Walking barefoot in the grass.

Putting lavender oil in my bath even when I didn't feel

worthy of self-care.

Those small things mattered.

They anchored me.

And in nervous system liberation, anchors are everything.

I leaned hard into my digital marketing business, because guess what?

Everyone was home.

Everyone wanted to get healthy.

And I had something to offer.

More money started coming in.

The purpose started showing up.

I was like, "Wait... is this what alignment feels like?"

It didn't feel like spreadsheets or business plans.

It felt like texting someone back from the bathtub and thinking, I can do this.

It felt like reclaiming tiny pieces of myself in between nap times and emotional spirals.

And then came the girl gang.

Before this, I chose friendships like armor.

People I could impress.

Circles that demanded performance.

I didn't know how to be loved in my mess, only in my achievements.

But something shifted in those early months. I stopped performing. I stopped filtering. I felt as if I had nothing else to lose.

And like magic, women appeared who didn't need me to be shiny or perfect.

They just wanted me real.

I naturally attracted friendships that matched this new version of me.

Raw. Honest. No BS.

Women who were also fresh out of situationships, marriages, and emotional trauma clean-up duty.

I remember taking my first Uber to meet them at a bar, which, let's be clear, was a whole event because I didn't even know how Uber worked.

We drank, we laughed, we danced, and then ended the night skinny dipping at 2 a.m. in our friend's backyard pool, talking about the last decade of our lives and how it all just burned to the ground for each of us.

And then, naturally, being the homebody I am, I died of a hangover and had life regrets for a solid 48 hours.

Another time, we aimlessly drove around during another COVID shutdown in my friend Sarah's giant SUV.

Shoutout to her ex-husband for owning a car dealership—that luxury bus was basically our chariot of freedom.

We blasted '90s music. Our wildest friend climbed into one of the car seats, buckled herself in, and started karaoke-ing Celine Dion with full conviction.

I think I peed my pants that night. Zero shame.

They accepted me, the raw, messy, newborn version.

No judgement. No trying to fix me.

Just complete, unconditional, ridiculous, sweaty, laugh-until-you-snort acceptance.

Was this what real friendship felt like?

The kind that didn't require you to abandon yourself just to belong?

The kind that stuck up for you in rooms you weren't in?

That reminded you who the f*ck you were when you forgot?

I hadn't felt that alive since my teens.

We were healing. Loudly.

"Strong female friendships increase resilience, improve mental health, and even help regulate stress hormones like cortisol."
— Psychiatry Research Journal

Translation?

Your girl gang isn't just fun; they're healing magic with matching tumblers.

There's actual science to support what we intuitively feel: friendship is medicine.

When women gather, oxytocin (the bonding hormone) rises, stress levels lower, and our sense of safety in the world strengthens.

This is primal.

This is ancestral.

Our nervous systems are wired for co-regulation. We're literally designed to heal in the presence of other safe, grounded humans.

So no, that wasn't "just a wild summer." That was collective healing disguised as chaos.

That was therapy in bikinis, breakthroughs over boxed wine, sisterhood in the rawest form.

After being stuck in a controlling, isolating relationship

for ten years,

Life had finally let me loose.

And I wasn't just walking into my freedom, I was sprinting in a crop top with a margarita in hand.

Breakdowns strip away everything fake.

The roles. The masks. The "shoulds."

And what's left?

The real you.

And she's spicy as hell.

I didn't know it at the time, but I was doing something sacred:

I was remembering myself.

Not the version of me who performed, achieved, or held it all together.

The one underneath. The one who had been silenced. Softened. Shamed.

And with every day that I laughed louder, cried harder, or said screw it and danced anyway,

I peeled back one more layer of survival, and finally started living.

Wrapped With Hope

So no, it wasn't polished.

It wasn't perfect.

But it was real.

And while I didn't know it at the time...

Those messy, rebellious, soul-shaking months?

They were the beginning of my becoming.

It didn't look like a journaling retreat in Bali.

It looked like boxed wine, breast pumps, midnight meltdowns, and borrowing someone else's WiFi.

But I wouldn't change a thing.

Because sometimes?

The soul work starts in sweatpants...

And ends in freedom.

It's not cute now, but just wait for the glow-up.

No-BS Reinvention Reflection: Breakdowns = Breakthroughs in Dirty Sweatpants.

1. What have I outgrown emotionally, mentally, or spiritually, but still keep clinging to out of fear? (This might sting a little—but it's the truth that sets you free!)
   Be honest. Not from a place of judgment, but from a place of clarity.

   _____

   _____

   _____

2. What parts of you did that breakdown reveal, shed, or awaken?
   (Anger, truth, rebellion, softness—name it.)

   _____

   _____

   _____

   _____

3. What would "rebellion mode" look like for you today? (Not reckless... just real. What does freedom feel like in your body?)

   _____

   _____

   _____

Mantra to steal

"I don't need to hold it all together to be powerful. I rise from the mess, bolder, louder, and more alive than ever."

Chapter 4
Quit Lying to Yourself, Babe

We gaslight ourselves more than anyone else ever could. We become the villain, the victim, and the master manipulator in our own story, all before breakfast...

Self-gaslighting is what happens when we internalize invalidation. We start dismissing our needs before anyone else can, not because we're broken, but because we've been conditioned to think we're "too much."

The Lie I Believed: I Don't Need Anyone (But Also, Do I Even Know How to Kiss Anymore?)

After my divorce, I told myself I was done with men. Done. No more heartbreak. No more shrinking myself. No more sacrificing my sanity so someone else could feel whole.

I was powerful now. I was free. I was giving full "I am woman, hear me roar" energy with a side of "don't even look at me if you can't handle me."

"All I need is me and my baby girls." I said it with my chest, and just a sprinkle of unhealed trauma.

And honestly? There was truth in that. I did rise from the ashes. I rebuilt my life. I found strength I didn't know I had. But here's the plot twist nobody talks about in the Strong Woman Handbook:

I was also scared sh*tless of ever being vulnerable again. Like, truly, terrified.

Re-entering the Dating World: Cue Existential Panic

At some point, I remember lying in bed thinking: Do I even know how to kiss anymore?

Should I... practice on my hand? Like we did in sixth grade at sleepovers when we were "preparing" for our futures as hormonally confused teens with lip gloss and braces?

The thought of being naked in front of someone new made me want to crawl into a burrito blanket and never emerge.

I felt like a 30-something virgin being reborn into a world where swiping right was a form of foreplay and ghosting was just part of the journey.

(Post-divorce dating isn't just awkward, it's dysregulating. When you've spent years in survival mode, even basic intimacy can activate a fight-or-flight response.)

All I knew was what my 21-year-old self knew: meet a guy at a bar, fall in love fast, get married, ignore the red flags, let the emotional bomb go off... you get the gist.

There was no "slow and conscious" in my love story playbook; it was full tilt or full crash.

And Then Came Brad.

Canada Day, 2020.

Mid-pandemic. Mid-identity crisis. Mid-rebuilding-my-entire-damn-life era.

The world was upside down, and I was clinging to my independence like it was my emotional support blanket. I had my girls, my boundaries, and, thanks to chronic stress and a divorce diet of adrenaline and nausea, my body was accidentally banging. (Which, if we're being honest, might be the unsung silver lining of the breakdown phase. KIDDING. Kind of.)

For the first time in months, I actually felt ready to do something out of my comfort zone, BIG TIME. Not just survive the day, but actually say yes to life again. Or at least say yes to Lana.

Now, Lana, let me paint you a picture, is what I lovingly refer to as my Chaos Curator. She's the kind of woman who always knows someone with a yacht, a mansion, a tiger, or all three. She radiates main character energy, has the kind of social circle that feels like a Netflix reboot of Gossip Girl: Cottage Edition, and somehow always has VIP access to people's backyards that are the size of city parks.

And at this stage of my life? That's exactly the kind of unhinged, life-is-meant-to-be-lived energy I needed.

So when she invited me to a "secret" Canada Day party, emphasis on secret, because, you know, global pandemic and all, and casually mentioned we'd be arriving by yacht... I didn't even blink. No kids this year. No ex-husband. No obligations. Just a woman on the edge of reinvention with a gut feeling that this was the start of something.

That morning, Lana rolled up with two of her goddess girlfriends, the kind of free-spirited, radiant women who somehow always smell like coconut and success. Meanwhile, I was wearing a ball cap, nursing emotional whiplash, and trying to hide the bangs I'd hacked off myself during what could only be described as a 2 a.m. post-divorce crisis. The contrast was... cinematic.

We got to the dock, and I swear, I entered an alternate universe.

There was music. Champagne. Strangers with veneers that glowed in the sun. A yacht so gorgeous I actually made a sound, like a confused, excited baby giraffe. I half expected someone to yell "SURPRISE! You're on a reality show!" and hand me a rose.

I did what I always do when I'm overwhelmed: I talked to everyone. I was a virgin to this version of life. Everyone fascinated me. Everyone felt like a new chapter. Like a shiny invitation to remember who I was before life started dimming the lights.

Shortly after, a pontoon boat pulled up beside us, and guess who was casually Sea-Dooing alongside it like a pandemic prince?

Brad.

It had been over a decade since I'd seen him. We were 19 the last time our paths really crossed, back when I dated his best friend and he dated mine. There was no grand romance, no teenage crush, no pining glances across a basement party. He was just... Brad. The funny, down-to-earth guy who felt more like a safe space than a spark.

But now? Seeing him again, barefoot on a Sea-Doo with that same goofy smile, something shifted. Not butterflies. Not fireworks. Something softer. Steadier.

It wasn't "Oh my god, I think I'm in love."

It was "Oh wow... I feel safe."

Like my inner wiring recognized something my brain hadn't caught up to yet.

He looked the same but different, older, grounded, like life had both softened and sharpened him in all the right ways. And when he waved at me like no time had passed at all, something in me exhaled. A version of me I hadn't met in years... came home for a second.

Naturally, I yelled, "B-RAD!" like we were in a teen drama from 2005. He looked up with his "no big deal, but kinda is" smile, and waved like he'd been expecting to see me all along.

We all eventually got to the shore where the cottage party was happening. And let me tell you, this wasn't your typical "crack a beer and light a sparkler" situation. This was the party.

Boats were everywhere. People were walking along the shoreline, music was bumping, folks were dancing on docks and hot tubbing on the deck like it was the Hamptons, all in blatant violation of every COVID restriction known to man. It was absurd. It was beautiful. It was the most alive I had felt in years.

And then... Brad pulled up. Again.

I ran over to him and gave him a big hug, you know, the kind where your whole body exhales? We did the usual "what's new?" catch-up, but something about it felt different. Safe. Familiar. Like maybe my soul recognized him before I did.

We separated for a bit, everyone was mingling, drinks were flowing, little white pills were being passed around like it was 1969 (don't worry, I stuck to Prosecco and poor decisions), and I just let myself be. Unfiltered. Unapologetic. Liberated.

By this point in the night, I was riding a champagne confidence wave, so naturally, I asked Brad to take me on a Sea-Doo ride. He didn't hesitate. He gunned it like a teenager with a need for speed, and I screamed with a mix of joy and mild regret.

At some point, he made me take the handlebars.

Reader, I almost killed us. Twice.

But he just laughed, not the condescending kind, the kind that says, "I've got you." It was thrilling. It was ridiculous. It was joy in its highest form.

We spent the rest of the night inseparable. Fireworks on the beach. Dancing barefoot. Laughing. Hot tubbing under the stars. It was one of those nights that feels like it was written for a movie montage, the kind with a chill indie soundtrack and slow-mo sparkler shots.

It didn't end until sunrise.

Brad ordered us a cab, yes, a cab, not a boat, which I'm pretty sure cost him the equivalent of a small mortgage, because we were an hour from civilization.

I collapsed into the backseat, physically drained and emotionally high on life. Before I stumbled into my house, I said something wildly inappropriate, which made him laugh out loud. He still had my number saved from when we were younger and said that he would text me.

I walked in the front door, collapsed face-first on my couch, and just whispered to myself, "WTF was that?"

Answer: that, my dear reader, was a plot twist wrapped in river water and spontaneity.

Little did I know, that ridiculous, reckless, sunburned day would become our anniversary. Not the kind with a calendar reminder or fancy dinner, the kind your soul bookmarks because it felt like a shift.

That was the day I reconnected with someone I already knew, and met the version of myself I had forgotten.

And isn't that what love really is?

Not just fireworks and hot tubs, but safety wrapped in surprise. Laughter wrapped in letting go. The kind of love that shows up in the middle of chaos and says, "You don't have to do this alone anymore."

Little did I know, that random, reckless, day would be the start of the safest love I'd ever know.

The Truth That Set Me Free

Spill time. I told myself I didn't need anyone because I was scared to need again. It wasn't just about romantic love; it was about trust. In others. In life. In myself.

Because if I really admitted what I wanted...

If I really told myself the truth...

I wanted connection.

I wanted softness.

I wanted a partner who didn't dim me but saw me, and stayed.

I wanted to be held without having to carry everything alone.

(We're wired for co-regulation. Even the most self-sufficient women thrive when they feel emotionally safe and mirrored by another nervous system.)

But for years, I told myself the opposite, that needing

anything made me weak. That wanting love again meant I hadn't healed. That choosing partnership would mean losing my power.

None of that was true.

I wasn't lying because I was dumb. I was lying because I was scared.

And sometimes, fear sounds a lot like wisdom when you're still healing.

(Wounds often disguise themselves as logic. They'll tell you you're being "smart" for not trusting. But really, it's your past trying to protect you from repeating pain.)

"The truth will set you free, but first it will piss you off."
— Gloria Steinem

That truth? That self-honesty? That radical clarity?

It will rattle your emotional circuitry.

It will make you sweat.

It might mean letting go of the identity you clung to in survival.

But on the other side of that truth is the life you actually want, not the one you settled for, or postured for, or pretended to be fine in.

So quit lying to yourself, babe.

Not because you're wrong.

But because you're finally ready for real.

(When you speak your real truth out loud, your brain literally reorganizes around it. You're not just thinking differently—you're rewiring.)

You can't build a life that turns you on if you keep gaslighting yourself into tolerating one that turns you off.

You say you're fine, but are you fulfilled? You say you don't need anyone, but are you secretly starving for intimacy, connection, safety? You say you're strong, but are you using independence to avoid vulnerability?

Here's your wake-up call:

Your next level doesn't need a mask. It needs your honest, messy, unfiltered truth. Power starts where your performance ends.

No-BS Reinvention Reflection: Unfiltered AF— No makeup, No mask. Just you and the truth.

1. What am I pretending not to want because I'm afraid it'll make me look weak?

   _____

   _____

   _____

   _____

2. Where have I turned self-protection into self-sabotage?

   _____

   _____

   _____

   _____

3. If I got radically honest today, what would I finally give myself permission to do?

   _____

   _____

   _____

   _____

Bold Reminder

Radical clarity is the first step
to reinvention.
If you want the life, the love, the
freedom, it starts by telling yourself
the freaking truth.
You're not too much. You're just not
meant to be diluted.

PART TWO: THE MESSY MIDDLE

Chapter 5
Choosing Yourself, Even When You'd Rather Choose Tacos

I've come to believe that our twenties are the years of learning how to choose ourselves.

They're messy.

Full of masks and moments where we abandon ourselves in the name of love, approval, or survival.

We shape-shift to be liked. We say "yes" when we're dying to say "no."

We settle, we overextend, we ghost ourselves.

And then one day, we wake up, and we don't even recognize who we are anymore.

That's when the real work begins.

Choosing yourself isn't always adorable or sexy or empowering in the moment.

Sometimes, it's lonely.

Sometimes, it's boring.

And sometimes, it's the only thing keeping you from falling apart.

By 2020, choosing myself was still relatively new to me.

Still uncomfortable. Still foreign.

I had to be deliberate about it, because my old ways? They loved to creep back in when my wounds were loud.

But I had done the work. I was healing. I was integrating.

And I refused to go back.

Summer was good to me.

Between custody schedules and pandemic lockdowns, I was either all-in as a mom, or out being reckless, loud-laughing with my girlfriends, or slowly learning how to feel playful again alongside Brad.

(Yes, that Brad. The same one I told myself I didn't need. The same one who cracked open a version of me I forgot existed. More on that later.)

And in between the chaos of lawyers, isolation rules, grocery shortages, and trying to keep myself physically and emotionally upright, I kept going.

There were moments when I felt like I was collapsing under the weight of it all.

Scream crying. Rage running.

I'll never forget when I sprinted in the pouring rain through Riverside South and collapsed into a random tree like a dramatic movie character on mushrooms.

It was absurd.

It was perfect.

It was the most healing thing I had done in weeks.

Fun fact: movement and crying are actually two of the body's most effective ways to release built-up cortisol. So that dramatic tree-hugging meltdown? Technically... neural recalibration.

That's not a breakdown, babe, that's a biologically accurate discharge of suppressed stress hormones. Also known as: healing, but make it cinematic.

Because choosing yourself doesn't always look like green smoothies and TikTok rituals.

Sometimes it's sobbing into your steering wheel.

Sometimes it's showing up in sweats and doing one small, meaningful thing: making a simple, nutritious dinner, going for that walk, saying "no" to the person who keeps crossing your line.

(Choosing yourself isn't always loud. Sometimes it's a whisper that says, "I deserve better," and a quiet unfollow.)

I wanted to give up. To shut down. To eat tacos and scroll memes until 2026.

But I didn't.

Because I knew if I let the fear and heaviness take the wheel, I'd miss the magic waiting just beyond the mess.

So I chose myself, imperfectly.

Some days I overdrank.

Some days I didn't eat at all.

Some days I danced in the kitchen.

Some days I journaled and felt powerful.

And some days I just... floated.

(Floating = freeze. And freeze doesn't mean failure. It means your body hit the brakes so you wouldn't fully crash. Respect the float.)

But through it all, I showed up.

For myself. For my girls. For the future that felt blurry, but worth it.

Self-Commitment Isn't Strict. It's Sacred. (Especially When the Light Feels Dim.)

I used to think self-discipline meant being harsh or rigid.

Now? I see it as an act of devotion.

To keep promises to my future self, even when present me is tired, snacky, and over it.

Choosing yourself means not skipping your needs when things get hard.

It's honoring your energy even when no one's watching.

It's saying, "I matter," without needing a reason.

(Neuroscience confirms: keeping small promises to yourself, drinking water, going to bed, writing the damn text, builds self-trust. And self-trust is the root of unshakable confidence.)

And yes, sometimes it means saying no to tacos.

(Or at least not using them to avoid your big life goals.)

Here's the thing no one tells you: sometimes choosing yourself isn't the loud, boss-babe moment on a vision board.

Sometimes it's closing your laptop early.

Sometimes it's letting yourself be average for a day.

It's unsubscribing from emails that make you feel not-enough.

It's saying, "I can't do that right now," without apologizing.

And slowly, miraculously, you begin to believe you're worth showing up for.

Your Energy Is a Bank Account (And You Can't Manifest on Overdraft)

I think of our energy like money in a bank account.

Some days, you're making big deposits, you slept well, had a great laugh, maybe even squeezed in a walk outside (or at least a really good coffee). Those moments fill your energy bank account, making you feel rich, capable, and ready to take on the world.

But then there are those days when you're stuck in back-to-back meetings, drowning in emails, or wrestling with that nagging inner critic.

Those moments? They're like sneaky withdrawals.

Suddenly, your account balance is low, and you're running on empty.

Signs your energy is in overdraft? You're irrationally crying over dishwasher tabs, doom-scrolling for validation, or fantasizing about fleeing the country to sell coconuts. Welcome to burnout.

That's why self-care isn't just bubble baths; it's boundaries.

It's rest. It's nutrition.

It's asking yourself, "What would the future version of me thank me for today?"

Even if present you is just trying to survive without

eating an entire bag of tortilla chips in bed.

(Let's reframe "lazy." What if lying on the couch watching Netflix while breathing like a potato is actually trauma-informed nervous system restoration? Because... sometimes it is.)

Also, fun fact from behavioral science?

Decision fatigue is real. Your brain has a limited number of quality decisions per day. That's why you snap over socks on the floor or forget why you walked into a room. Your internal state is tired.

Realignment Happens in the Micro-Moments

You don't have to overhaul your life to choose yourself.

You just have to notice when you've ghosted yourself, and come home again.

One walk.

One glass of water.

One boundary.

One tear you actually let fall.

That's the real self-care.

That's the reinvention.

Forget the 12-step glow-up. Real growth is saying,

"No thanks" when your body says stop, even if your calendar says go.

Realignment can happen at 2 p.m. in traffic or 11:42 p.m. in your kitchen with a Post-It note that says "Hydrate Queen".

Every time you choose presence over perfection, you rewire your brain to see safety in softness.

That's the neuroscience of self-compassion.

But What If Choosing Yourself Still Feels Unnatural?

You might feel guilty.

You might feel like a fraud.

You might even hear that voice whisper, "Who do you think you are?"

That's not your intuition, that's your default mode network.

It's your brain trying to protect your identity as it's always known it.

(In plain English? Your body's command center sees your glow-up as a possible threat. This is why stepping into your power can actually trigger anxiety.)

So if you feel resistance? You're not defeated.

You're just growing.

Growth doesn't always feel like a pep talk. Sometimes it feels like nausea.

Sometimes it feels like exhaustion.

Sometimes it feels like mourning the version of you who put everyone else first.

But she's proud of you for choosing something better.

When Choosing Yourself Triggers Other People

Here's the plot twist nobody warns you about:

When you stop abandoning yourself, people who benefitted from your self-abandonment might not like it.

Suddenly, your boundaries seem "selfish."

Your silence becomes "rude."

Your growth? "Too much."

But their discomfort is not your responsibility to soothe.

(According to family systems theory, any shift in behavior, even healthy ones, can destabilize the dynamics people have relied on. This is called homeostatic resistance, and it's why standing in your power can sometimes feel lonelier before it feels freer.)

You're not doing it wrong.

You're just finally doing it the right way for you.

Energy Leaks That Are Quietly Draining You

Let's not pretend. You might be choosing yourself...
but also:

- Replaying a convo from three days ago
- Overexplaining your "no" to people who don't deserve it
- Letting the group chat decide your worth
- Or holding your pee for 6 hours out of habit

All of it = emotional overdraft.

It's time to patch the leaks.

Patch one and suddenly you have the energy to make that phone call, write the resume, move your body, eat something nourishing.

The shift doesn't start with a glow-up.

It starts with a choice.

5 Small Ways to Choose Yourself Today

1. Water before coffee.

2. Say "I need a minute" when your body's screaming.

3. Leave one thing undone.

4. Ask, "What do I need right now?" and give it to yourself.

5. Put your hand on your heart and say, "I've got you."

Choosing yourself today doesn't mean you'll never fall back into old patterns. It just means you'll catch yourself quicker and love yourself louder when you do.

Let's Pull Back the Curtain

Some days you will absolutely still choose tacos.

And memes.

And 47 minutes of couch scrolling when you should be glowing.

But that doesn't erase your growth.

Healing isn't linear.

Self-love isn't rigid.

And choosing yourself doesn't mean you always want to—it just means you remember to.

Even on the messy days.

Even when you'd rather choose tacos.

No-BS Reinvention Reflection: Every time you don't abandon yourself, you rewrite the story.

1. Where are you overspending your energy on things that don't serve you?

    _____

    _____

    _____

    _____

    _____

2. What's one small but powerful choice you can make this week to reinvest in yourself?

    _____

    _____

    _____

    _____

    _____

3. What's the next brave move I'm willing to make, today, not someday?

    _____

    _____

    _____

    _____

    _____

The Choice That Changes Everything

The hardest choices aren't the ones
that feel impossible.
They're the ones that feel optional,
the ones you'd rather skip because
"tacos" sound easier.
Choose you, every time.
Even when it's inconvenient.
Even when it feels easier to hide.
That's the choice that
changes everything.

Chapter 6
Burn The Rulebook
(It Was Trash Anyway)

Be nice. Be small. Be available. Be perfect. Be likable.

Girl, be quiet.

Those were the rules. I didn't write them, but I sure as hell lived by them.

Most of us were handed a silent script before we even knew we were reading it. Be agreeable. Don't make waves. Smile more. Stay busy. Don't be too emotional. Work twice as hard to be taken half as seriously.

And whatever you do, never, ever need anyone.

I wore independence like a badge of honor, not realizing it was also a total trauma response.

Hyper-independence is often misread as strength, but it's actually the regulation system saying, "We don't trust anyone enough to help."

WHO THE HELL WROTE THESE RULES?

These rules didn't come from your soul; they came from generations of survival. Family patterns. Cultural messaging. Capitalism. Instagram quotes in pastel fonts. They came from moms who never rested, dads who never cried, bosses who wanted you to do "more," and boys who only liked you if you didn't need them too much.

And I can confidently assume, most of the rules were written by people who had no idea what the hell they were doing either.

When He Walked In, My Inner Wiring Walked Out

When Brad entered my life, he broke every unspoken rule I didn't even know I still believed.

He was soft. Gentle. Joyful. He held my hand like it was the most natural thing in the world. He offered to rub my back and didn't expect anything in return. He made dinner plans. Texted back. Showed up. Emotionally. Consistently. Without keeping score.

And although my heart whispered, "This is what you asked for," my body screamed, "RUN."

(Because when you've been trained to associate love with unpredictability, consistency can feel suspicious.

Safety isn't just something you receive. It's something you have to learn to stay with.)

I remember sitting there thinking:

"Why is he being so nice? What does he want? Should I offer to pay? Sleep with him? Bake something? Explain myself? Prove I'm worth it?"

I didn't know how to just receive.

I'd been so conditioned to hustle, fix, prove, and do, I forgot what it felt like to be nurtured. I had confused feminine power with weakness. I had confused love with sacrifice. I had confused emotional safety with something you earn instead of something you deserve.

Brad's kindness wasn't the problem.

It was just... foreign.

(Sometimes the "ick" is your inner child not recognizing safety because she's only ever known pain disguised as love. Healing means staying long enough to show her the difference.)

When Life Tests Your New Rules

It's one thing to burn the rulebook.

It's another thing entirely to live without it.

That was the real test.

I had been doing the healing work. Rewriting the rules. Practicing softness.

But the Universe doesn't just hand out gold stars—she hands you a pop quiz when you least expect it.

Just a few months into my relationship with Brad, you know, the era when things are supposed to be light and fun and full of flirtatious texts and spontaneous weekend getaways, I found myself staring down a moment I could've never prepared for. The kind of moment that doesn't come with a script or manual. Just real emotions. Real fear. Real intimacy.

We had already agreed: more babies weren't in the plan. My cesarean had revealed that my uterine lining was dangerously thin, and I had made peace with the idea that it wasn't safe for me to carry again. Brad knew this walking in. It gave him pause at first, sure. But we had our hands full with my two daughters, and we had love, laughter, chaos, dreams. One day, maybe we'd explore other options. But for now, we were good.

Until I missed a period.

Three days late. Then four. And I knew.

Tender breasts, off energy, my body was whispering something I didn't want to hear. I booked an appointment "just to check." And yep. I was pregnant.

Cue emotional whiplash.

Shock. Panic. Disbelief. Then came the ultrasound.

And with it, devastation.

It wasn't viable. It was ectopic. The pregnancy had implanted outside the uterus. Dangerous. Life-threatening. Emergency status. No time to process.

They gave me abortion pills. I cried all night.

They didn't work.

So then? Chemo.

Yes, chemotherapy, injected to stop the growth.

You're talking to a woman who preaches neural network regulation and treats her body like a sacred temple. And here I was, about to be injected with actual chemo drugs in a cold room covered in warning signs.

I was shaking. Pale. Numb.

But the male nurse who held my hand that day? An angel. Wrapped me in a blanket. Talked me through it like I wasn't just a patient, but a person.

I went home hollow. Sick. Soul tired. For weeks, I had blood tests every 48 hours.

The fetus kept growing.

The hormones stayed high.

I kept waiting to feel okay again.

The days that followed were a fog of fatigue, grief, and a strange kind of stillness.

I wasn't just physically sick. I was soul sick.

There was no funeral, no closure, no language for the kind of grief I was carrying.

It felt too complicated, too early, too medically complex for most people to understand.

But for me? It was real. The moment I saw the word "pregnant," my body and brain had already started attaching alternative outcomes.

I couldn't even have more kids, and now that choice had been taken from me again, and in what felt like, the most violent, clinical way possible.

I was grieving something I hadn't planned, but had quietly started loving anyway.

And that's the kind of grief no one really talks about.

It was the death of possibility.

I remember standing in the shower, forehead against the tile, and whispering, "Why does my body feel like the enemy?"

My hands, once nurturing and mothering, now felt foreign.

There was shame. Rage. Confusion. Loss.

And under it all, a quiet question I couldn't shake:

What kind of woman was I, if I couldn't do what a "real" woman was supposed to do?

That narrative was old, I knew that. But it still lived inside me.

Because when you're taught your worth is linked to who you care for and what you can create, any limitation can feel like a personal failure.

But Brad didn't let me spiral alone.

He reminded me, gently, and over and over, that this wasn't the end.

That I was still whole. Still worthy. Still wanted.

Even when I couldn't stop crying. Even when I lashed out.

Even when I couldn't hold it together, or hold him, or even hold myself.

And for the first time, I didn't retreat into hyper-independence.

I didn't armor up or hide how much it hurt.

I let go of the old rule that said I had to do it all alone, and I let myself be cared for.

This chapter of our relationship, born out of crisis, gave us a kind of intimacy that years of dating apps and slow-build love stories never could.

There's a moment in every healing journey when the body says, "This is new, this is terrifying, and I'm going to need you to breathe through it."

And this was mine.

I was receiving love in a way that felt undeserved because the rulebook had taught me that worthiness was transactional.

But here he was, loving me with no terms and no timelines.

Just presence. And patience. And Pho soup.

That's the kind of rewriting no journal prompt can prepare you for.

Because it's one thing to believe you're worthy of love.

It's another thing entirely to sit in the darkest season of your life, let someone see you, and not flinch.

And it's even harder to believe they'll stay.

But he did.

And with each quiet moment, each middle-of-the-night "are you okay?" check-in, each forehead kiss, my neural pathways started to recalibrate.

This wasn't love that needed proving.

This wasn't performance.

This was safety, in its most sacred form.

And somehow, that ectopic pregnancy, the thing that broke us both, also built something we couldn't have forged any other way.

It became the cornerstone of our relationship.

Not because we wanted it.

But because we survived it.

And not as two individuals who made it through, but as a partnership that chose to grow deeper in the wreckage.

And that? That's when I knew the rulebook really was in ashes.

Because I didn't just rewrite the story,

I lived it.

Who Are You Without the Hustle?

See, I had spent most of my life playing the Giver.

Not just as a role, but as a full-blown identity.

It made me useful. Needed. Liked.

But underneath that identity?

A fear of abandonment.

A belief that love had to be earned.

And a nervous system addicted to emotional chaos.

(There's actual research behind this: we call it anxious attachment. It wires your brain to equate intensity with intimacy. If love feels calm, you assume something must be wrong.)

That role, the over-functioning, over-performing, self-sacrificing woman, was what brought me to rock bottom in the first place.

And the wildest part? I thought it was noble.

But the more I look back, the clearer it becomes:

My standards for others were non-existent.

My standards for myself were sky high.

And I called that balance.

(If you're bending over backwards to meet everyone's needs while resenting them for not doing the same, that's not balance. That's emotional burnout in cute lipstick.)

Tell me, have you ever found yourself:

- Thanking someone profusely for doing the bare minimum?

- Feeling guilty for resting?

- Feeling like you owe someone for simply being decent?

- Doing everything... and then resenting everyone for letting you?

That's not love.

That's a pattern.

And patterns are meant to be broken.

Rewrite the Rules (Yes, All of Them)

Here's the thing no one warns you about:

When you finally receive the love, support, softness, or safety you've always longed for...

your body's control center might glitch like a 2004 Dell laptop.

You'll want to run.

Sabotage it.

Over-explain.

Or convince yourself it's "too good to be true."

(That's not you being dramatic. That's what happens when your body holds on to the past longer than your mind does, mistaking peace for danger. In healing, calm feels boring, even unsafe, until your body starts to believe that safety doesn't always end in betrayal.)

You're not a project. You're a masterpiece in motion.

And you're just unlearning a story you didn't write.

I remember the exact moments I had to intentionally stop fighting the good:

The first time I was offered physical affection without expectation.

The first gift I didn't feel guilty for receiving.

The trips.

The morning texts just to say "Have a good day."

The protection, real protection, from someone who spoke beautiful things about me behind my back.

It was foreign.

I had built a life around the belief that my light triggered the people around me.

So I learned to dim it.

To shrink.

To stay small enough not to disturb anyone's comfort.

(Many women were raised to believe being palatable was more important than being powerful. So we tone ourselves down until we don't recognize our own voice anymore.)

But I remember all of it.

Not because it was epic or extraordinary.

But because each moment rewired a piece of me that had forgotten what it felt like to be cherished, without needing to perform.

Those moments were pivotal.

They still are.

I stopped auditioning for affection.

I stopped hustling for crumbs and calling it a feast.

I stopped believing I had to earn ease, joy, and love.

(And that's when life started to flow. Because the Universe doesn't respond to desperation, it responds to alignment.)

I started letting life love me back.

And I burned the rulebook.

(Spoiler: it was trash anyway.)

A Quick Note For You, Reader

If you've ever felt like:

- You owe people something just because they're nice to you

- You need to "earn" rest, kindness, or love

- Softness is weakness

- Hustling is your personality trait

...you are not flawed. You were just playing by outdated rules.

So here's your permission slip to stop asking for permission.

Your softness isn't the opposite of strength. It's the evolution of it.

You don't have to prove anything to be worthy of love.

You don't have to shrink to be safe.

You don't have to perform to be chosen.

This is your invitation to stop apologizing for taking up space.

To receive, fully.

To feel, deeply.

To let good things happen... without sabotaging them out of habit.

Let's Part for Now With This:

You don't need to prove your worth by burning yourself out.

You don't have to hustle for the love you were born to receive.

You are not here to be convenient.

You are here to be held, seen, and true.

Light the match.

Burn the rulebook.

Write your own damn script.

The women before you survived so you could break the pattern.

The women after you?

They'll thrive because you did.

No-BS Reinvention Reflection: I don't owe anyone my exhaustion. I receive with power. I rewrite the rules.

1. What rules have you been following that make you feel small, stuck, or secretly resentful?

_____

_____

_____

_____

_____

2. When was the last time you let someone give to you... without apologizing for it?

_____

_____

_____

_____

_____

3. What would happen if you stopped proving and started receiving?

_____

_____

_____

_____

_____

Unapologetic Mantra:

I don't beg for breadcrumbs
anymore. I sit at the damn table
I built.
My softness is sacred. My worth isn't
up for negotiation.
I don't need to perform to be loved. I
need to stay rooted enough
to receive.

Chapter 7
Your Boundaries Aren't "Too Much." They're Just Not For Everyone

---

If they think your boundaries are rude, they were benefiting from your lack of them.

Let that marinate.

Boundaries aren't an attack.

They're a filter.

And when you finally install one? Whew. Watch who starts glitching.

I remember after my second baby, Amelia, my time was short, and my patience was thinner than the postpartum hairline I pretended wasn't receding.

At that point, I felt like I was doing everything, for everyone, with nothing in return. Fatigue was high. Resentment? Higher. I was stretched thinner than the elastic on my 6-month-old nursing bra.

I was working part-time as a dental hygienist, full-time as a digital marketer, and breastfeeding like it was my third job. (And yes, I weirdly miss it now. Hormones are wild.)

On top of that, I was providing emotionally, physically, financially, spiritually... hell, if someone had asked, I probably would've thrown in a free root canal just to keep the peace.

To say I was exhausted would be an understatement. Honestly, I think I blacked out for the majority of my children's younger years.

There were days I'd realize I hadn't eaten, peed, or even looked in a mirror until 4 p.m. And if I did catch a glimpse? She looked like she had been on a three-day survival hike with a toddler duct-taped to her hip and a double-shot of espresso running through her veins.

Here's the kicker: most of my friends didn't have kids yet. So while they were out brunching, bottomless mimosa-ing, and "just popping by for a girls' weekend," I was elbows-deep in diapers and deadlines, running on pure adrenaline and shutdowns.

I was still playing by the outdated rulebook that said, "I take the kids 24/7, you do you, and I'll just silently implode in the corner."

So leaving the house alone? A full-blown fantasy.

Grocery shopping without a toddler meltdown? Luxury.

Silence? A forgotten dream.

And the guilt? Ohhh, the guilt.

Every time a group text came in, "It's so-and-so's birthday! You better be there!!", I felt like I was drowning in invisible ink.

I always knew I wasn't going. It was just me, myself, and I.

But I didn't know how to say it.

Because saying, "I can't come, I'm barely holding my life together with breastmilk and broken boundaries," would've shattered the perfectly filtered portrait I'd spent the last five years curating.

The marriage.

The motherhood.

The "she's got it all together."

But I didn't have it all together.

I had spreadsheets, sippy cups, and an internal compass one group chat away from combustion.

You know that feeling when it seems like you're disappointing everyone around you?

Like no matter how hard you try, someone's side-eyeing your choices, whispering about what you should be doing, and waiting for you to show up in a way that you physically, emotionally, and spiritually can't?

Yeah... that was me.

I was drowning in the pressure to make everyone happy while barely staying afloat myself.

No boundaries. No transparency. No village that even remotely understood what I needed.

Just me, slowly disintegrating under the weight of invisible expectations I never agreed to carry.

And to be clear, it wasn't anyone's fault.

People can only meet you as far as they've healed.

They can only support you to the depth of what they've experienced.

And we already know: in your twenties, that emotional toolbox?

Wobbly. Incomplete. Missing half the screws.

You're lucky if you've got a Phillips head and a half-empty wine bottle.

Everyone around me was doing their best with what they had,

And so was I.

But best doesn't mean sustainable.

And I was at a breaking point.

So What Do Boundaries Actually Mean?

Boundaries are not walls.

They're not ultimatums.

They're not about being cold, distant, or "too much."

Boundaries are clarity.

They're self-respect in action.

They are the standard you set to protect your energy, your peace, your mental health, your family, and your nervous system.

They are how you teach the world to treat you.

NEUROSCIENCE NOTE 🧬

Chronic boundary violations keep your body in fight-or-flight mode. When you're constantly saying "yes" when you mean "no," your brain interprets that as a threat. Your amygdala gets louder. Your cortisol rises. Your logic shuts down. Boundaries re-engage the prefrontal cortex, the calm, rational part of your brain, so you can show up with clarity instead of collapse.

And in that season of my life, the blurry, burnout, postpartum survival zone, I had none.

But somewhere between breastfeeding at 2 a.m. and laying on the bathroom floor while answering a group text I had no business being in, something shifted.

I realized I had spent so much time trying to be understood... without ever demanding it.

So much time over-explaining, justifying, shrinking, performing, all while dying inside.

That version of me was constantly available. Chronically overwhelmed. And secretly resentful.

Because I wasn't being honest about what I needed.

Hell, I didn't even know what I needed.

How I Started Creating Boundaries

It didn't happen in a single moment.

It wasn't a dramatic, slam-the-door-and-block-everyone-on-social-media kind of thing (although... tempting).

It started small:

- I stopped replying to texts right away, without guilt.

- I said no to events I didn't have the capacity for, even if it made people uncomfortable.

- I communicated clearly, not defensively.

"I'm in a season where I don't have the same flexibility. Please don't take it personally."

- I stopped explaining my exhaustion like it needed a permission slip.

- I started expecting people to meet me with compassion, and if they couldn't? That told me everything I needed to know.

Life tip: Use the 3Rs to build boundaries:

Recognize where your energy is leaking.

Reclaim your priorities without guilt.

Reinforce your new standard, not through force, but through consistency.

I stopped chasing understanding and started requiring it.

And let me say this as clearly as I can:

If someone gets upset about you honoring your capacity...

They were never respecting you to begin with.

When I Really Learned Boundaries

Summer 2021.

My first real trip away from my babies, and honestly, one of the most unforgettable weeks of my life.

Brad, my Libra through and through, thrives on beauty, balance, and "doing the most" (in the best way). He lives for adventure. Travel is his therapy. And since COVID had us grounded from international flights, he poured his energy into planning the most luxurious domestic escape he could dream up: a 7-day trip to Whistler, BC, just the two of us.

We're talking bikes, hikes, hot tubs, mountain views, wine, lakes, and... ziplining with my dad.

Yes. Brad's first time meeting my father involved being strapped to him, flying 600 feet above a canyon on Canada's largest zipline.

If that's not Libra-level drama-meets-charm, I don't know what is.

We did it all, whitewater rafting, hiking into alpine lakes, biking trails that made my thighs scream, and ending every evening with a glass of wine, the mountains painting a masterpiece around us.

And yet... I almost missed the magic.

Even though I had carefully planned the girls' schedule, staying with Nana on "my" days and with their dad on his, I hadn't protected my energy.

I was still responding to texts.

Still explaining myself.

Still caught in emotional loops that should've been locked up in a vault back home.

The first two days of our trip felt like I was dragging my mental baggage up a mountain.

Brad could feel it. I could feel it.

We were in paradise, but I was mentally glued to my phone.

Brad didn't say much. He's never one to make a scene, but I remember the look on his face when I vented (again) about a message I shouldn't have even read.

It was the look of someone quietly wondering, "Are we really here... or is your mind still there?"

That was my boundary-breaking moment.

Right there in Whistler.

I muted the number.

Let my mom be the amazing Nana she is.

And decided, for the first time in over a decade, to unplug not just from tech, but from the identity of the always-on, always-fixing woman I thought I had to be.

And let me tell you: it was bliss.

That version of me, laughing, resting, flirting, exploring, truly living—she was the woman I'd been missing.

And boundaries? Boundaries gave her back to me.

We came home from that trip lighter. Not because life magically changed; it didn't. There were still co-parenting tensions, sticky texts, and toddler meltdowns waiting at baggage claim. But I had changed. I had seen what it felt like to actually rest in love. Not earn it. Not perform for it. Just... be in it.

And that version of me, the one who came back from Whistler, glowing, steady, sun-kissed, and a little smug? She wasn't going back to performing for proximity.

Not long after that, we knew it was time. One year into dating, learning to be playful again, a heck of a lot of growth, and a few emotional software updates later, we decided Brad should meet the girls.

Which sounds so simple, but if you've ever introduced your kids to someone new, you know... it's like giving someone a key to your entire emotional universe. I had done so much work to protect their peace, and mine, I wasn't about to let anyone waltz in with charm and empty promises.

But Brad didn't try to impress. He didn't push. He met them exactly where they were, on their terms, with full presence and zero pressure. He made pancakes. He played. He let them take the lead. He showed up as a safe space, not a substitute.

And then? Around one year after that moment, we made another big move.

I finally got bought out of my marital home.

He sold one of his rental properties.

And we bought our first home together.

Not out of obligation. Not to check a box.

But because we were both finally building something from alignment, not survival.

And you know what made it possible?

Boundaries.

Hard conversations.

Saying no to people who didn't understand.

Saying yes to ourselves even when it makes others uncomfortable.

That home wasn't just drywall and paperwork.

It was proof that when you stop leaking energy to the wrong places, the right life builds itself around you.

And it's damn beautiful.

The New Standard

I realized that if you don't like where I'm at,

If you can't offer grace when I'm stretched thin,

If my boundaries feel like rejection instead of protection...

Then you don't deserve access to this version of me.

Because this version of me is sacred.

She has survived. She is healing.

She is choosing herself unapologetically.

And from now on? That is the bare minimum.

Redefining Boundaries

Boundaries are not walls.

They're not punishments.

They're not dramatic ultimatums with a side of guilt.

They're doors, with locks, handles, a welcome mat, and a peephole.

You get to decide who comes in, who stays out, and who gets blocked and saged out of your energetic foyer.

Boundaries say:

- "I love you, but I won't abandon myself to keep you comfortable."

- "This is the version of me I'm protecting. If you can't respect that, there's the door."

Friendships & Relationships

Some people won't understand your boundaries because they were never planning to meet you halfway.

They liked the version of you that said "yes" when you meant "no."

The one who bent, broke, and smiled through the resentment.

Setting boundaries in friendships will feel weird if your friendships were built on your self-betrayal.

Setting boundaries in love will feel harsh if your relationships were built on overgiving and under-receiving.

You are not "too much."

You were just surrounded by people who expected too little from themselves.

The Guilt Is Normal, You'll Survive It

Yep. Some people will get uncomfortable.

They'll call you selfish.

They'll ghost you.

They'll say you've changed.

And they're not wrong.

You have.

You're no longer performing for proximity.

You're no longer people-pleasing to avoid abandonment.

You're no longer the easy version of you they could guilt into submission.

What No One Tells You

Figuring out your boundaries will cost you the life you're currently living.

It might cost you your favorite friendships.

Your "I know they mean well" people.

Your convenient situationships.

But it will gift you peace.

Clarity.

Power.

And alignment.

That's the trade.

And it's worth it.

No-BS Reinvention Reflection: Repeat after me, "I'm not hard to love, I'm just no longer easy to use"

1. Who drains your energy the fastest, and why do they still have access to you?

_____

_____

_____

_____

_____

2. Where do you need to say "no" more boldly?

_____

_____

_____

_____

_____

3. Write a boundary you've been afraid to set—and what would it free up if you did?

_____

_____

_____

_____

_____

Boundary Blessing

May you trust yourself enough to
disappoint others. May you protect
your peace like a sacred ritual. May
you remember: clear is kind,
and your capacity is not up
for negotiation.

Chapter 8
Blame It On The Inner Child
(But Also...Hug Her)

Ever completely lose your cool over something tiny? Like a short text, "K.," and suddenly you're spiraling, sweating, spiraling, and spiraling some more? That's not your rational adult self. That's your 5-year-old inner child, confused and abandoned all over again, just with better Wi-Fi.

That's what shadow work is really about. It's not about staying stuck in the past; it's about understanding how the past still lives in your body.

What is Shadow Work, really?

Shadow work is the process of uncovering and healing the parts of yourself that you've tucked away, rejected, or avoided. These are your unspoken fears, old survival strategies, unmet emotional needs, and beliefs you picked up before you could spell "self-awareness."

Think:

- People-pleasing

- Always needing to prove yourself

- Avoiding conflict at all costs

- Shutting down when you feel vulnerable

Shadow work isn't about becoming someone new. It's about reclaiming all the parts of yourself you've been at war with.

In psychology, Carl Jung coined the term "shadow" to describe the unconscious parts of our personality that our ego doesn't identify with. These parts aren't bad— they're just hidden.

Why It Matters

Because what you don't heal, you repeat.

You'll attract the same patterns, the same types of people, and the same emotional roller coasters, thinking it's fate when it's really just unhealed pain looking for resolution.

Shadow work gives you the keys to:

- Respond with clarity instead of reacting from wounds

- Make conscious choices rather than repeating emotional reflexes

- Become a safe space for yourself

My Wake-Up Call Came After the Calm

It wasn't in the chaos that I broke.

It was in 2022, when things were finally good.

Brad and I were building something beautiful. The girls were safe. Our home felt whole.

My business was thriving.

And for the first time in years, I felt ahead, emotionally, financially, spiritually.

I genuinely believed I had made it.

I thought I had healed.

I was finally living the life I had fought so hard to create.

But here's the thing about healing your inner child:

You don't get to skip the parts that scare you.

You don't get to bypass the dark just because things look bright.

Out of nowhere, the fear returned.

That old, familiar panic, like a ghost I hadn't quite laid to rest.

Anxiety. Dread. The feeling that everything could slip away at any moment.

My fear of losing control. Fear of abandonment. Fear of the what-ifs, louder than ever.

And I was pissed.

Confused.

Like... why the hell am I back here?!

I thought we did this already?!

Had all my "healing" been a performance?

Had I simply decorated my pain with good habits and called it growth?

I didn't want to go back.

I didn't want to feel it all again, the abandonment, the rejection, the raw vulnerability of being cracked open.

But something deeper inside me knew:

This was the work I couldn't skip anymore.

Fun fact: The brain doesn't know the difference between a past emotional threat and a present one unless you actively create safety in the moment. **That's** why your boss's passive-aggressive email feels like your childhood all over again.

The Bathtub Breakdown (aka My Spiritual Ambush)

I had known for a while that I wanted to become a life coach, but I wasn't ready to take the leap.

What I was ready for? Quiet healing. Something for me.

So when I came across an ad for "Become a Certified Spiritual Life Coach," it sparked something.

Not because I wanted to teach others.

But because my soul whispered, "This might be the path back to yourself."

I signed up for the course, expecting tools and checklists.

What I got instead?

A 30-minute meditation to heal your inner child.

Okay, Universe. I hear you.

I lit a candle. Slid into the bathtub. Hit play.

Figured I'd meditate for a bit and check the healing box. Simple.

Within minutes, I was laid out in that tub like a starfish, arms and legs wide, heart cracked open.

And then the tears came.

Full-body, shaking, Niagara Falls tears.

The kind that makes you wonder where the hell it's all coming from.

I thought I wasn't "an emotional person." I wasn't someone who cried often.

And yet, there I was, sobbing into bathwater, asking myself:

What is happening to me?

Why is this wrecking me?

Am I really this unhealed?

The answer was yes.

Not in a shameful way, but in a revealing way.

Because I had finally stopped running.

I let her, the little girl inside of me, speak.

And once she felt heard?

She didn't hold back.

This is the moment that broke me open.

Not in a way that ruined me, but in a way that rebuilt me.

I didn't want to go back to the beginning.

But the truth is, that's where the gold was buried.

That's where the healing lived.

That's where she was waiting.

Neuroscience shows that emotions stored in the body often re-emerge when we enter states of rest or safety, like baths, massages, or even walks in nature. Stillness can be triggering, not because you're broken, but because your system finally feels safe enough to release.

My Story, with Compassion

Let me be clear, this isn't a chapter to bash my parents. This is a chapter about understanding their humanity so I could reclaim my own.

My mom grew up in foster care and joined the military to escape a system that never protected her. She taught me strength and structure, but softness? Emotional safety? She didn't have a blueprint for that. And that's okay.

She was learning how to survive while parenting. She was young. Unparented. Figuring it out as she went.

My dad? My light-filled, wild-hearted, live-in-the-moment father. He loved life deeply, but consistency and emotional grounding weren't in his toolset.

He brought joy, humor, and presence, but at a time when emotional regulation wasn't something men were taught. He, too, was navigating life with the tools he had.

At 12, when my parents divorced and my mom got posted across the country, I was left to emotionally fend for myself.

Not because they didn't love me. But because they were still learning how to love and support themselves.

They were doing the best they could. And that matters.

But so does what I needed.

We all did the best we could with what we knew. And today? They're my best friends. They've become the most incredible Nana and Grandpa to our kids, playful, generous, full of love. We're all still learning. But we've grown. And I'm so lucky to call them mine.

When Love and Safety Weren't Modeled...

Lorin Krenn says it beautifully:

"Our mother is meant to teach us how to love.

Our father is meant to teach us how to feel safe and secure.

And if we were not modeled that, then our deepest work lies in learning how to love fully, and how to return to safety inside our body."

That quote cracked something open in me.

If your mother did not show you how to love, your heart will carry armor around it.

If your father did not show you how to feel safe and secure, then creating safety in your body is your work.

I had to face it: My heart was armored. My nervous system was always bracing.

And it wasn't anyone's fault. It was just what was passed down.

And now, with awareness, we get to choose what we pass on next.

Bonus brain nugget: Our early attachment patterns shape how we respond to stress in adulthood. That "fight, flight, freeze, fawn" response? It's not drama— it's data.

Forgiveness, Without Excusing

"This is not about blaming your mother or father.

It is about seeing their limitations clearly, and choosing not to carry them forward.

The cycle ends with you." – Lorin Krenn

Forgiveness is the decision to stop waiting for someone else to fix what happened, and instead, choosing to give yourself what they couldn't.

Forgiveness doesn't mean reunion. It means release. You don't need a group hug; you need a clean boundary.

The Work Begins With You

You don't need a retreat in Bali to begin. You just need honesty, compassion, and a willingness to sit with your truth.

Start here:

1. Notice your patterns. What keeps repeating?

2. Get curious. Ask: "Where did I first feel this way?"

3. Talk to your inner child. Out loud. Lovingly.

4. Journal. Be raw. Be messy.

5. Create safety. Through breath, boundaries, rituals, and rest.

Not sure where to start? Try writing a letter to your 5-year-old self. Tell her what she needed to hear. Then read it out loud. (Yes, even if you feel ridiculous. Healing rarely looks cool.)

You're Not Broken, You're Brave

Your inner child didn't get a choice in how it started.

But you do get to decide how it continues.

You get to break the cycle. You get to become the safe, loving, whole woman she always needed.

She doesn't need you to be perfect. She needs to know you won't abandon her again.

The cycle ends here, with love.

She Comes With Me Now

You can now find me looking into the mirror, into my own eyes, and saying:

"I love you. You are safe. You are divinely protected."

I visualize myself walking hand-in-hand with the younger me.

She's barefoot, curious, wide-eyed, and I whisper, "I got you."

I picture hugging her tightly. Letting her feel held in a way she never got to be.

And when I cry now, I no longer see that as weakness. I see it as a reunion.

Every tear is a thread that stitches us back together.

She comes with me wherever I go.

Because she is me.

And I am her.

So if you take one thing from this chapter, let it be this:

She didn't get a choice back then.

But you do now.

Choose Her.

Powerful One-Liners Your Inner Child Needs to Hear:

- You didn't have to earn love, you were always worthy of it.

- It wasn't your job to keep the peace.

- You were not "too sensitive." You were deeply in tune.

- Your needs were never too much.

- You didn't imagine it. That was hard.

- You shouldn't have had to figure that out alone.

- It's okay to rest now. You're safe.

- You were never broken. Just unheard.

- You're allowed to take up space.

- You don't have to be perfect to be loved.

- You can start again. You always get to try again.

- You deserved gentleness. You still do.

No-BS Reinvention Reflection:

Let's get radically honest with the little girl inside of you, the one still waiting to feel safe, loved, and seen.

No sugar-coating. No spiritual bypassing. Just deep truth, compassion, and real AF self-leadership.

1. What emotion was I shamed for as a child, and how is that still showing up in my adult relationships?

   _____

   _____

   _____

   _____

2. What BS generational belief am I done carrying?

   _____

   _____

   _____

   _____

3. What does true safety feel like, not in theory, but in my nervous system?

   _____

   _____

   _____

   _____

End-of-Chapter Affirmation

I am no longer abandoning the girl I used to be. I choose her. I soothe her. I lead her. And together, we rise.

Chapter 9
PAUSE, BREATHE, DON'T PANIC

When the Hustle Breaks and the Soul Finally Breathes

September 2024.

A month I will never forget.

It was the paradox of everything I had dreamed of... and everything falling apart in the same breath.

On the outside?

Everything looked golden.

My brand was finally hitting that momentum I'd been grinding for over six years. Goss Magazine, yes, THE Goss Magazine, reached out asking to feature me. A literal vision board moment that once felt so far-fetched it made me laugh.

(Shoutout to that psychic from 2019 who said, "I see you in Goss." At the time, I thought she sneezed.)

I was in the middle of a rebrand. Photoshoot booked,

website being rebuilt, a whole new vibe coming to life.

I felt seen, aligned, on track.

My business finally looked the way it always felt in my heart.

"This is it," I whispered to myself one night, staring at my laptop like it was my newborn child.

"All those sleepless nights... the doubting, the pushing, the praying... this is the breakthrough."

And then, just like that, it all shattered.

THE EMAIL THAT UNRAVELED ME

Two days after my Goss shoot.

Two weeks before my magazine submission was due.

Ping.

An email hit my inbox like a slap from the universe.

The U.S.-based health and wellness company I had partnered with, the one that had freed me from dental hygiene and gave me financial stability, was pulling the plug on all digital marketers.

Thirty days.

That's how long I had before my income would drop to $0.

No warning.

No conversation.

Just a cold, corporate mic drop.

The air left my lungs.

My fingers trembled.

I walked out to Brad, reading the email aloud in a voice I didn't even recognize.

I sobbed.

"What the hell am I going to do?!"

This wasn't just a job.

This was my PLAN A.

My freedom. My soul's work. My ticket OUT of an industry that had quietly been eating away at me.

This company gave me purpose. A team. Community.

And now... it was over.

THE PANIC LOOP

For the next few weeks, I barely ate. Barely slept.

I was in a full-body spiral.

Cue the late-night Google binges:

- "Signs of burnout."

- "Should I go back to hygiene?"

- "Universe, are you mad at me?"

I thought about canceling the Goss magazine piece.

What was I even promoting now?

Who was I without the brand I had built?

This, my friends, was what we call an identity crisis.

And it was... humbling. Violent. Necessary.

It felt like spiritual whiplash.

But looking back? It was divine redirection with glitter bombs and a megaphone.

#HUSTLECULTUREISCANCELLED

I was still booked to go on a cruise with that same company, a reward trip I had earned with grit, late nights, and genuine heart.

Every cell in my body wanted to cancel it.

"F*ck them," I told myself. "I'm not going."

But then something in me whispered:

"No. Go. But don't hustle on that boat. Don't make it content. Don't 'network.' Go be a human."

So I did.

I showed up not as a brand, but as a woman in transition.

I watched the sunrise. I sat by the water. I unplugged.

And for the first time in years, I didn't feel the need to prove anything to anyone.

I was just Jessica.

Not the mentor. Not the marketer. Not the woman with all the answers.

Just... me.

And Brad, bless his larger than life ways, made it a trip I will never forget.

At this point, he could see I was breaking. Not the kind of break a nap could fix. The kind where your entire being doesn't know what mask to wear anymore. Where every version of you feels like it's crumbling and none of them feel safe. I was teary eyed at random moments, zoning out in conversations, and spiraling between "maybe I'll delete everything" and "maybe I'll start a new brand by Monday.

Every day on that trip was carefully and quietly curated by a man who knew I needed wonder. I needed beauty. I needed joy that wasn't attached to efficiency.

He booked the most stunning restaurants, each one

with candlelit tables, ocean views, and fresh Sea-Doos that made me audibly moan in public like someone who hadn't eaten in weeks.

He brought me teas with the perfect amount of coconut cream, before I even opened my eyes.

He made sure every detail felt luxurious, not for show, but for restoration.

And the Bahamas? She understood the assignment.

Brad planned an entire adventure day that made my body forget what depletion even was.

We Sea-Dood across the open ocean, just us and the wild, turquoise water, wind whipping through my hair, salt on my skin, no notifications, no deadlines, no "what's your five-year plan?" Just freedom. Just presence. (With a side of Sharks.)

Later that afternoon, we E-biked across Paradise Island. I'm talking full-body, quick, wind-in-your-face, laughing-until-you-can't-breathe kind of fun. We stopped for fresh coconuts, explored tiny side streets filled with vibrant culture and sunshine, and found ourselves on hidden stretches of beach that looked like they were pulled from a travel magazine. The kind of places you imagine you'll go when you finally slow down... and then never do. But this time, I did.

I did it barefoot, sun-kissed, and supported.

That trip wasn't just beautiful. It was the first time in a long time I exhaled without guilt.

Not because it was extravagant, but because I didn't have to earn it.

Because I was allowed to exist in joy without being result driven.

Brad didn't need me to be "on."

He didn't need me to teach, inspire, or perform.

He just needed me to be present. Alive. Real.

And for the first time in a long time, I felt like a woman again, not a brand, not a provider, not a machine in mascara, but a human, held by love, softened by rest, and reminded that I don't have to grind to be worthy of alchemy.

STILLNESS ISN'T WEAKNESS. IT'S STRATEGY

Here's the thing nobody tells you about stillness:

It's not easy.

It's not whimsical.

It's not "peaceful" or straight out of a lifestyle blog.

It's itchy. It's triggering. It's loud.

Stillness makes you sit with the ghosts you've been outrunning.

And in that sitting... in that quiet, sacred, terrifying pause, you finally hear the truth:

> **You've outgrown the version of you that was just surviving.**

I wasn't meant to rebuild what broke.

I was meant to build something new.

STILLNESS

According to neuroscience, activates the Default Mode Network in the brain, essential for introspection, self-awareness, and creativity. So when you think you're doing nothing? Your soul is blueprinting the next level. Quietly. Powerfully.

THE REBIRTH (AKA HOLY S***, THIS IS WORKING?)

Just two weeks after we returned from our trip, the magic started trickling in.

Emails.

Opportunities.

DMs that felt like divine breadcrumbs.

A message from the Speakers Bureau of Canada, an opportunity I had applied to MONTHS earlier and totally forgotten about.

They wanted to interview me.

I got the gig.

I needed income again, so I made the scary decision to return to dental hygiene part-time.

But here's the catch:

My youngest daughter, neurodivergent, wasn't reliably in school, and my schedule needed to be tight.

I asked for a $20/hour raise at the office I had worked at for 14 years.

New Management said no.

I didn't cry.

I didn't beg.

I said: Cool. This is my permission slip to walk away.

And then...

I got a DM on Instagram from another Jessica THAT EXACT DAY.

"Come work with us," she said.

I told her what I needed.

She said: "Done."

I interviewed on Friday.

Got everything I asked for: the hours, the days, the respect.

It was like the Universe said,

"Now that you've stopped settling, let me show you what's possible."

MIC DROPS

* You are allowed to pivot without a polished plan.

* You are allowed to leave what no longer serves you, even if it once saved you.

* Stillness doesn't mean nothing's happening. It means everything is happening, beneath the surface.

IF YOU'RE IN A SEASON OF UNCERTAINTY, READ THIS TWICE:

The breakdown isn't the end.

It's the opening.

Your stress response system knows before your mind does. Listen to it.

Loyalty is beautiful... until it becomes the thing that keeps you stuck.

When the door slams shut, trust that something softer is trying to make its way in.

HOW TO FIND YOUR WAY BACK TO YOU:

1. Unfollow 50 people who drain you. (Start with that girl who makes you feel like you need a new kitchen and a thigh gap.)

2. Block out one day with zero commitments. No guilt allowed.

3. Journal like your soul depends on it. Because it does.

4. Get in water: shower, bath, ocean, lake. Water heals. (Bonus: it drowns out other people's opinions.)

5. Breathe. No, really. Deeply. In for 4, hold for 4, out for 8. (Your vagus nerve will thank you.)

6. Say no to something out loud. Even just once. Extra credit if you do it with a smile.

7. Remind yourself: You're allowed to change your mind, your brand, your pace, your whole damn life.

CLOSING THOUGHTS

If you're reading this and your world feels like it's unraveling,

LET IT.

You're not off schedule.

You're off autopilot. (And that's a win)

You are in the sacred space between endings and beginnings.

I didn't plan the pivot.

But it's exactly what I needed.

Because the truth is:

I wasn't being punished.

I was being redirected.

And what came next?

Was better than anything I could have forced

No-BS Reinvention Reflection: Before you rush into your next "what's next," pause. Let this chapter sit in your bones. Now ask yourself the real questions.

1. If I stopped waiting for permission, what version of me would I finally become? No fluff. No filters. What have you been secretly craving to do, be, or become... if fear wasn't in the driver's seat?

_____

_____

_____

_____

_____

_____

2. Where am I still hustling for validation instead of healing for peace?
Explore where you're over-performing, people-pleasing, or forcing momentum, and what it would feel like to just rest without guilt.

_____

_____

_____

_____

_____

_____

3. What had to break down in order for me to
   break through?
   Get honest. What ending or loss forced you to
   finally face yourself? What clarity or truth came
   from the chaos?

   _____

   _____

   _____

   _____

   _____

   _____

Mantra to Carry Forward

If it broke you, it taught you. If it
freed you, it changed you. But if it
shook you to your core, that's the
sign it was part of your reinvention.
Not everything that ends is a loss.
Sometimes it's divine eviction.
Trust the unraveling. Write this
down. Highlight it. Tattoo it on your
nervous system.

Chapter 10
Awkward Phase—But Make It Iconic

They'll whisper, "She's different now," like it's a betrayal.

But we didn't come here to stay the same. We came to evolve, unapologetically.

2025 came in hot, like wildfire meets identity crisis.

And if I'm honest, the end of 2024? Still feels like a blackout.

Not the party kind. The deepest self kind.

The kind where your whole inner calm center short-circuits and says,

"Yeah, we're not doing that anymore."

I had been gripping on to survival by the edge of a burnout-colored thread.

Everything that once made sense, didn't.

Everything I built felt heavy.

And everything I thought I wanted? Suddenly sounded like it belonged to someone I didn't recognize anymore.

But somehow, through the chaos and confusion, this new year felt different.

Grounded. Unfamiliar, but peaceful.

Like meeting a version of myself I hadn't seen in years.

The one who wasn't constantly trying to prove she deserved to rest.

Welcome to the Safety Era

(Where Nothing Sparkles, But Everything Stabilizes)

So there I was, re-entering the world of dental hygiene.

Yep, again.

Now before you roll your eyes (because I definitely rolled mine at first), let me say this:

Was it my dream job? No.

Did it feel like my purpose? Also no.

But did it keep the lights on, the fridge stocked, and my children clothed in their suspiciously expensive taste for neutral-toned outfits? Yes.

And more than that, it gave me something I hadn't felt in a while: belonging.

My team welcomed me with open arms and even bigger smiles.

They noticed the little things. Thanked me often.

Laughed at my quirky ways. Let me rearrange systems and still said "thank you" instead of "sit down."

That alone was revolutionary.

After years of being the leader, the coach, the content-creator-mom-hustler-scheduler with 17 tabs open in my brain at all times, it felt oddly healing to just be a teammate.

No one needing me at all hours.

No one expecting a webinar.

No inbox full of crisis.

Just... clean teeth and kind coworkers.

Honestly? Iconic.

Here's the science-y part: In psychology, this kind of reset is known as "role relief." When you've spent too long being the responsible one, the fixer, the performer, stepping back into a low-stakes role allows the nervous system to recalibrate.

Studies show that chronic over-functioning (being "the one holding it all together") keeps the sympathetic nervous system activated. Hello, cortisol overload. But role relief? It restores clarity, stabilizes your mood, and even reduces systemic inflammation.

So yes, gloves, fluoride, and a Spotify playlist called "calm but vibey" were, surprisingly, part of my rebirth.

And honestly? Sometimes awakening doesn't look like therapy and epsom salts. Sometimes it looks like predictable shifts, clean scrubs, and knowing your next paycheck will clear. Stability became sexy. Routine became revolutionary.

Returning to hygiene may have felt like a step back to some, but for my body? It was finally a step in, into regulation, rhythm, and rest.

And besides, it was just temporary. Seasonal. Cyclical. Exactly the way life intends everything to be.

Hosting My First Workshop (And Mildly Spiraling Afterwards)

As if the universe wanted to throw in a little "growth spurt" for good measure, I hosted my first workshop around the same time.

The name?

Hustle Culture is Cancelled: From Now On We're Relaxing Our Nervous Systems and Getting Into

Energetic Alignment With the Intended Outcome

Yes. That was the literal title.

Was it a mouthful? Yes.

Did it scream "I'm healing and high-functioning"?
Also yes.

It wasn't a workshop. It was a full-blown soul sermon.

Part TED Talk, part nervous breakdown.

I poured everything I had into that event, the lessons, the breakdowns, the tools, the breakdowns again (because one wasn't enough).

I wanted it to feel warm, cozy, and real.

I didn't want anyone to leave inspired. I wanted them to leave regulated.

The vibes were unmatched:

- Dairy-free, gluten-free snacks (gut health queens only)

- Herbal teas that healed your trauma with every sip

- Floor cushions, candles, a curated playlist

- And my dear friend Julie, a numerologist who dropped bombs like Taylor Swift on tour

It was magical.

And when it was over, I crashed harder than a toddler after a birthday party.

Not because it went badly—it went amazing.

But I realized quickly that the energy required to hold that space wasn't something I could sustainably give.

Here's a gentle truth:

Just because you're good at something doesn't mean it's good for you.

This is called empathic burnout.

When your gift is also your trigger, your body will eventually wave a red flag, even if the world is clapping.

I heard mine loud and clear.

According to trauma-informed psychology, holding emotional space for others without enough self-regulation or recovery time can lead to a type of secondary trauma. Your nervous system starts responding as if you lived through everything you're holding for others. And if you're not careful? That space you created to heal others can slowly become the one that breaks you.

Turns out, even beautiful things come with energetic price tags. And the more deeply you feel, the more intentional you have to be about what you absorb. Emotional labor doesn't show up on paper, but your body keeps the receipts.

Reintroducing Myself... To Myself

That season, the soft, slow, unspectacular days that followed, became sacred.

I was learning how to just be.

And I'll be honest: I sucked at it at first.

I was a hustler in recovery.

Addicted to adrenaline.

Obsessed with "what's next."

Hardwired to believe that silence meant failure.

But something was shifting.

Some days, I wrote my book with tears in my eyes and my heart in my hands.

Some days, I shared something honest online that made a stranger feel seen.

And most days, I just sat in the stillness, sipping lukewarm tea while my daughter told me an unnecessarily long story about a fox again.

And for once, that was enough.

Brad noticed.

The girls noticed.

They told me I laughed more.

That I wasn't as short-tempered.

That I was actually with them now instead of floating above the room in a cloud of guilt and mental checklists.

Ouch.

And also... thank you.

I needed to hear that.

Sometimes your expansion doesn't come from pushing, it comes from pausing. Reawakening didn't require a grand performance. It required presence. It required being boring on purpose. And slowly, the woman underneath the overachiever began to reintroduce herself.

Turns out, presence is medicine, and it works both ways.

When your neurobiology shifts into parasympathetic regulation (the rest-and-digest mode), your relationships improve. You're able to co-regulate with the people you love. Which means: when you're calm, they feel it.

Especially kids.

The Rise of the Boundary Queen

This era birthed a whole new version of me:

The boundary queen. The vibe protector. The no-texts-after-7 guardian of peace.

I became less available, but more present.

Less social, but more soulful.

Less "yes," but more hell yes.

If it wasn't aligned with my nervous system, it was a no.

If it felt forced, heavy, or obligatory, it didn't make the cut.

If the energy was off, I hit mute. Or block. Depending on the offense.

I wasn't mad. I wasn't bitter.

I was just done pretending everyone deserved access to me.

Let me be clear: I love people.

I just don't love being energetically mugged by them.

According to Dr. Nicole LePera, boundaries are not walls; they are clarity.

They teach others where we end and where they begin.

And when we finally set them, everything in us exhales.

Mine did. And then some.

Boundaries, from a somatic lens, are not just behavioral, they're biological self-protection. When you set a boundary, you're telling your autonomic system:

"I've got you. I won't override you anymore."

And that? That changes everything.

Energetic leaks are real. And every yes you give out of guilt becomes a slow erosion of your self-trust. Boundaries aren't selfish—they're sacred. They remind your system what safety feels like. And that safety? It becomes the soil for your future self.

Toronto: The Plot Twist That Rattled My Nervous System (and Ego)

Then, the email came.

An invite to compete in a motivational speaking challenge in Toronto.

The winner would receive $3,000 and paid speaking gigs.

Apparently, someone had seen my content and thought, she's got it.

My first reaction? Pride.

My second reaction? Panic.

(And mild gastrointestinal distress.)

This would be my first solo trip in YEARS.

No kids. No partner.

Just me, my stage outfit, and enough essential oils to open a wellness boutique.

I prepped like a woman on a mission.

Speech? Rehearsed.

Flight? Booked.

Sweat glands? Fully activated.

I kept telling myself, "Do what scares you. The magic is in the risk."

Meanwhile, my mind was screaming, "No, the good stuff is at home with chamomile tea and your dogs."

The High of the Stage... And the Hangover After

The day came. I flew. I arrived. I didn't die.

(That alone felt like a win.)

When I got on stage, something clicked.

I told my truth. My story. My pain and my power.

I laughed. They laughed. I cried. They clapped.

And when I got off stage, I felt alive.

This is it, right?

This is the moment. This is where I'm meant to be.

But then...

Then the crash came.

The come-down.

The hollow echo.

The realization:

To pursue this full-time means leaving the very life I had just fought so hard to rebuild.

The travel. The pressure. The ego.

The approval addiction.

All of it would drag me back to a version of myself I had just buried.

So I asked myself:

Am I chasing my calling... or chasing the clapping?

Do I want to speak... or do I just want to be seen?

There's a difference between purpose and performance.

One fills your soul. The other empties it slowly while feeding your ego.

And in that quiet come-down, I realized something else: the stage didn't give me my voice; my healing did. The mic was a mirror, not a destination. And I refused to lose myself again just to feel seen.

Redefining Power. Reclaiming Peace.

I used to think the stage was the highest form of purpose.

Now, I see it differently.

Maybe power doesn't always wear heels and hold microphones.

Maybe it wears slippers and reads bedtime stories.

Maybe it builds peace instead of platforms.

I still believe in my voice.

But now I believe in my silence, too.

Because the woman I'm becoming doesn't need to be famous to be impactful.

She just needs to be honest, with herself, first.

Becoming unrecognizable isn't scary.

It's powerful.

So, if you're in your awkward phase right now, the one where you're shedding the old but not quite sure what the new looks like yet, don't rush it.

Don't run back to what's familiar just because the silence feels uncomfortable.

Don't shrink just because you're misunderstood.

And don't apologize for being the woman who finally stopped abandoning herself to make others feel safe.

This chapter of you might be messy. Unpolished.
A little quiet.

But make no mistake: this is where your power is born.

Not in the applause.

Not in the climb.

But in the sacred, subtle moment you finally said:

"I choose me now."

And trust me...

That version of you?

She's not awkward.

She's becoming legendary.

No-BS Reinvention Reflection: For the woman outgrowing who she used to be and is no longer apologizing for it.

1. What does your "awkward phase" look like right now, and can you own it instead of rushing through it? What if this version of you is more iconic than polished ever could be?

   _____

   _____

   _____

   _____

2. Where are you still trying to earn your rest, your peace, your softness, instead of just claiming it? What would change if you decided you no longer need to prove your worth through exhaustion?

   _____

   _____

   _____

   _____

3. What version of you are you trying to keep alive, just because it makes other people more comfortable? Are you willing to let her rest so the real you can rise?

   _____

   _____

   _____

Little Reminder for the Road

I don't owe anyone an explanation for my peace, my glow-up, or my bedtime. I set the vibe now, and if that makes me "different," good. That was the assignment.

Chapter 11
Nothing's Working and
I'm Still Showing Up. (Send Snacks!)

"First, nothing seems to change.

Then suddenly, everything does.

That's the magic of neuroplasticity.

That's the miracle of quantum physics.

Do not quit before the neural pathways solidify.

Do not quit before energy turns to matter.

Don't give up before the magic happens"

- Let's Train the Brain

When nothing's working, your skin's breaking out, and Mercury's in retrograde for the 17th time, you've officially entered: The Messy Middle.

This is the part where most people quit.

The part where the scale doesn't move.

Your pants still don't button.

You feel bloated, moody, tired, and discouraged, and every cell in your body screams, "SEE?! I knew it. Nothing works for me."

Let me tell you something I wish someone had told me sooner:

The plateau is where your identity starts to shift.

It's not in the glow-up montage or the "after" photo.

It's in the unsexy consistency when everything feels like it's standing still, and you still show up.

That's what I want to talk about here:

What it really looks like to rebuild your life through your health.

Not seamlessly. Not overnight. But with intention, commitment, and a whole lot of snacks. (Healthy kinds with a side of cheesecake!)

Your Health Is the First Domino

We know this, you can't build a beautiful life on a burnt-out body.

I used to think mindset came first.

That I could just think my way into transformation.

But here's the hard truth:

If your gut is inflamed, your hormones are wrecked, your blood sugar is on a rollercoaster, and you're chronically dehydrated, your mind doesn't stand a chance.

Let's science that up real quick:

Studies show that 95% of serotonin (your mood-stabilizing neurotransmitter) is actually produced in the gut, not the brain. So if your gut is inflamed, your mindset is swimming upstream with bricks in its pockets.

Health isn't just about the number on the scale.

It's your base. Your foundation. Your home.

And I didn't truly take my power back until I decided to build that home from scratch, habit by habit.

So I made a promise to myself back in October 2018.

One new habit a month. No pressure. No extremes. Just one non-negotiable at a time.

That's how I lost 60 pounds.

Healed my gut.

Came off a decade of anxiety meds.

And started to feel like a person again.

Let's break them down. One by one.

No fluff. No filters. Just what actually worked.

THE HABITS THAT CHANGED MY LIFE

1. 10,000 Steps Per Day

Why it matters:

Walking is the most underrated form of physical AND mental therapy.

Seriously, you don't need to do CrossFit in the rain while crying to get results.

What it supports:

- Blood sugar regulation
- Lymphatic drainage (your body's detox system!)
- Digestion
- Cortisol reduction
- Mood elevation
- Creativity stimulation

SCIENCE DROP 💩

A 2021 study in JAMA Network Open found that people who walked at least 7,000 steps per day had a 50–70% lower risk of early death. That's not a cute Facebook ad stat. That's your longevity calling.

What it did for me:

At first, it was just "get out of the house and avoid snapping at my kids."

Then it became my moving meditation. My time to think, to breathe, to process.

There were days I'd cry during my walk, and others when I'd leave with five new business ideas.

It helped me move stuck energy, physically and emotionally.

Pro tip:

You don't need a treadmill or a perfect time block. I used to do loops around the kitchen while on Zoom. It still counts. JUST WALK.

2. 20 Minutes of Weighted Exercise

Why it matters:

Muscle is metabolically active tissue. That means the more you have, the more calories you burn at rest.

Benefits:

- Regulates insulin
- Balances hormones (especially for women 30+)
- Supports bone density and joint health
- Helps manage anxiety by increasing dopamine and serotonin

SCIENCE DROP 🧖

Muscle mass declines about 3–8% per decade after the age of 30. Lifting weights literally keeps you from turning into a cranky couch blob with sore knees.

What it did for me:

It gave me structure and discipline when my life felt chaotic.

And every time I thought, "I can't do this," I'd finish a set and realize, I just did.

That kind of confidence bleeds into every area of your life.

Pro tip:

No fancy gym needed. I used two dumbbells and YouTube or a workout app. (Bless the algorithm.)

3. 1 Gallon of Water Per Day (Yes, Really)

Why it matters:

Water is not just hydration. It's hormonal regulation. It's cellular renewal. It's... your brain juice.

Dehydration Symptoms (aka me in 2016):

- Fatigue

- Irritability

- Cravings

- Headaches

- Brain fog

- Dull skin

What it did for me:

Once I committed to hydration, I had fewer headaches,

less bloating, and even fewer sugar cravings. It's like my body stopped screaming because I finally gave it what it needed.

Pro tip:

Get a giant bottle you love and name it. I named mine Sheila. You don't forget to bring Sheila. Sheila is loyal. (I got mine off Amazon! It was inexpensive and had the time of day labeled which kept me on track.)

4. 1 Page of Personal Development Daily (or Audible)

Why it matters:

Neuroplasticity = your brain's ability to rewire and it is VERY real. Even one page a day can begin shifting your mental loops from "I'm stuck" to "I'm growing."

What it did for me:

It kept me focused on who I was becoming, not who I had been.

Some days I read a page and underlined half of it. Some days I threw it at the wall.

But every single day, it was a reminder that growth was happening, even when life felt still.

Pro tip:

Don't overthink the book. Just choose something that speaks to the YOU you're becoming, not the you you're trying to fix.

5. Speak Kindly, About Others and Yourself

Why it matters:

Words carry vibration.

Speaking harshly (even casually) sends stress signals through your nervous system.

SCIENCE DROP 📖

Research in psycholinguistics shows that self-talk affects emotional regulation, problem-solving, and behavior. Translation: your words either reinforce peace or chaos.

What it did for me:

It made me conscious of how much of my energy was being wasted on negativity.

When I shifted my language, my relationships softened, my confidence grew, and my anxiety reduced, dramatically.

Pro tip:

If you wouldn't say it to your child's face, don't say it to yourself in your head.

6. Intermittent Fasting (16:8)

Why it matters:

Fasting gives your body time to digest, detox, and reset your metabolism.

Benefits (when done correctly):

- Improves insulin sensitivity

- Boosts human growth hormone

- Reduces inflammation

- Supports cellular repair

What it did for me:

It taught me to eat intentionally, not reactively.

I had fewer cravings. Better energy. And best of all, my digestion healed. (After YEARS of bloating, cramping, and "what the hell did I eat?" days.)

Pro tip:

Read Fast Like A Girl by Dr. Mindy Pelz.

Start slow. And always break your fast with protein + fat first, not sugar or carbs. (Yes, even the gluten-free donut.)

7. Meditation (In Literally Any Form)

Why it matters:

Meditation isn't about perfection. It's about presence.

Nervous System Benefits:

- Lowers cortisol

- Boosts immune function

- Improves focus

- Increases gray matter (your brain's control center for emotions!)

What it did for me:

It gave me a moment to just exist, no expectations, no productivity.

I learned to sit with discomfort. To feel instead of suppress.

And it taught me how to listen to my body, not override it.

Pro tip:

Don't make it complicated. Some days I sat in silence. Some days I meditated in the bath. Some days I just laid in bed and did deep breathing. It all counts.

8. Cutting Out Alcohol Completely

Why it matters:

I wasn't a heavy drinker. I was a social drinker. A glass of wine with friends. A cocktail at the lake. A couple drinks on a business trip to take the edge off.

But here's the truth: even one or two drinks would leave me anxious, edgy, and nauseous for days afterward. Every. Single. Time.

No matter the occasion, I always regretted it.

What it did for me:

In March 2024, I decided I was done. Alcohol just wasn't worth the aftermath anymore, the 2 a.m. wakeups with a pounding heart, the emotional spiral for no reason, the way my body felt like it had been hit by a truck even after "just a few."

Since cutting it out completely, I sleep better. Think clearer. Feel stronger. My gut healed faster. My confidence came back. My energy stopped tanking by 2 p.m. every day.

Most importantly? I don't second-guess myself anymore. I feel present, like actually present, in my own life.

Science says:

Alcohol disrupts your brain's GABA and glutamate systems, the two neurotransmitters responsible for calming your nervous system and regulating mood. So that "relaxed" buzz? It's a short-term trick that often leads to long-term anxiety once those systems rebound.

What it could do for you:

If you're someone who drinks "casually" but deep down knows it's not sitting right anymore... this is your permission slip.

You don't need a dramatic story to justify walking away from something that doesn't serve you.

Sometimes the biggest transformations start with the smallest, most honest choice: I deserve to feel good.

And alcohol, even just socially, is standing in the way of that.

Final Thoughts: The Power Is in the Practice

You want to know what really changed me?

Not the weight loss. Not the healed gut. Not the before-and-after photos.

It was becoming a woman who kept showing up for herself, even when nothing was working yet.

This chapter is called "Nothing's Working and I'm Still Showing Up" because I was.

Bloated? Showed up.

Tired? Showed up.

Stressed, puffy, hormonal, irritated? Still. Showed. Up.

Because your body?

It hears consistency.

Not perfection.

Not punishment.

Just presence.

If you're reading this mid-spiral, mid-bloat, mid-burnout, let me say this:

You're not failing. You're rebuilding.

And if it feels hard, that's not a sign to stop.

That's a sign it's working.

Now grab your Sheila, take a lap around the kitchen, and remember...

Healing isn't a sprint.

It's a series of small, loving decisions stacked daily.

And you, my love, are showing up.

That's the kind of woman who doesn't just change her life.

She rewrites it.

No-BS Reinvention Reflection:

This isn't just about writing things down; it's about finally getting honest with yourself.

These prompts are here to crack something open.

To help you stop waiting for the just right moment, and start becoming the woman who shows up anyway.

Get real. Get clear. And don't hold back.

1. What's one small, loving thing you can commit to daily, even if it feels pointless right now?

   _____

   _____

   _____

   _____

   _____

   _____

2. Which habit from this list feels the most doable, and what would your life look like if you stayed consistent for 30 days?

   _____

   _____

   _____

   _____

   _____

   _____

3. Where are you confusing discomfort with failure? Could this be your messy middle, not your dead end?

_____

_____

_____

_____

_____

_____

Take This With You

You don't need to be flawless.
You just need to keep showing up,
bloated, tired, unsure, overwhelmed,
and still willing to take one step.
Because showing up when it's hard?
That's where your power is built.
That's where the transformation
begins. That's where the woman
you're becoming is born.
So if all you did today was drink
some water, take a breath, and
decide to try again tomorrow?
You're doing it right.

Chapter 12
The Universe Isn't Ghosting You— She's Just on Divine Timing

This isn't up for debate.

The Universe is not ignoring you.

She's just out here re-staging your entire life like an overcommitted theatre director yelling, "Places, people!" while you're in the wings wondering if you've been forgotten.

You're not being ghosted, babe.

You're being guided.

But I get it.

You ask for a sign, and instead of angelic clarity, you get a weird dream about your ex, a coffee spill on your white shirt, and 12 Instagram ads for therapy.

You're like:

"Excuse me, Universe? I asked for guidance, not a nervous breakdown in chunky heels."

But that's the thing, the spiritual signs?

They rarely show up with glitter, glamour, and a talking bush like in a Bible story.

They whisper.

They nudge.

They make you notice things that shouldn't matter, but do.

Like... 4:44.

When My World (Officially) Ended

December 30th, 2019.

That was the day my marriage legally ended. The reality? It ended quietly years before.

Emotionally, energetically, spiritually. The lights were on, but no one was home, and the foundation had been slowly crumbling like gluten-free banana bread left in the oven too long.

When the final signature hit the page, though?

It still gutted me.

No one prepares you for the moment you become a "single mom."

No one tells you how loud the silence gets in a shared custody schedule.

No one teaches you how to divide a life.

But also...

No one tells you that this kind of collapse might be the divine scaffolding of a completely new structure.

I didn't know it then.

I just knew I was devastated, confused, and barely functioning while polishing people's mouths and pretending like I wasn't spiraling.

The Day I Met 444

It was a random weekday. I was walking a patient out.

The Clock said: 4:44 p.m.

I paused and stopped right in my tracks.

Something about it hit different. I got chills.
My stomach flipped.

"What the hell was that?"

I didn't know anything about angel numbers. I wasn't fully "woo-woo" yet. I was barely functioning.

But I Googled it anyway.

And boom.

444 = You are guided. Supported. Watched over. Stay

the course. Don't give up.

You could've told me Carrie Underwood herself wrote that message and I would've believed it. Because it felt like it was for me.

I started seeing it everywhere.

Receipts. License plates. Email timestamps.
Random texts.

It wasn't a coincidence—it was confirmation.

And I began to realize...

The Universe wasn't ghosting me.

She was just making sure I noticed the breadcrumbs before dropping the whole damn loaf.

Signs vs. Synchronicities: What's the Difference?

Signs

- Definition: A direct message or symbol that stands out and feels meaningful.

- Example: Seeing 11:11 on the clock, finding a feather after asking for a sign, hearing a specific song that aligns with something you were thinking about.

- Energy Behind It: Often sent by your guides, the Universe, or your higher self to gently redirect, reassure, or encourage you.

- How It Feels: Subtle but powerful. A nudge, a knowing, or a sudden stillness.

- Purpose: To guide, validate, or show you that you're supported, especially during transitions.

Synchronicities

- Definition: Meaningful coincidences that align with your inner world in spooky-perfect timing.

- Example: Thinking of someone and they text you seconds later. Talking about a book and it shows up on your feed.

- Energy Behind It: Synchronicities are your energy reflected back to you, like mirrors from the universe.

- How It Feels: Like a wink from the cosmos. Chill-inducing. Heart-opening.

- Purpose: To show you're aligned and attuned, vibrationally connected to what you're calling in.

Final Thought:

Signs are like whispers from the universe: "We see you. Keep going."

Synchronicities are like full-body winks: "You're in the magic. Don't stop now."

But What If You're Not "Spiritual"?

Cool.

You still have a soul.

Whether you track moon phases, pull oracle cards, or just say "I get a bad vibe from Chad," you're tapped in.

Spirituality isn't about memorizing mantras or staging your living room with 12 kinds of sage.

It's about awareness.

Ever said, "I was just thinking about you," when someone texts?

Ever had a dream that came true?

Ever walked into a room and felt something was just... off?

Yeah. That's not random. That's resonance.

SCIENCE EVEN SUPPORTS THIS ☑

The Reticular Activating System (RAS) in your brain acts like a filter, noticing patterns that match your subconscious focus. It's why when you're thinking of buying a white SUV, you suddenly see 37 of them. The signs were always there; you're just now attuned.

Why Your Timeline Isn't Late, You're Just Early

Let me be fully transparent.

I've ugly cried in the front seat of my vehicle more times than I can even count.

I've journaled at 2 a.m. like I was submitting an emotional thesis.

I've pulled angel cards like a desperate girl pulling receipts after a bad date.

And still didn't get the clarity I wanted.

Because here's what I now know:

You don't get the blueprint before the leap.

You get the bricks as you walk the path.

Every detour, heartbreak, "WTF" moment? It's divine calibration.

Your delay isn't denial—it's development.

You're becoming the version of you who can carry what you're asking for.

The one who doesn't fumble it when it arrives.

The one who knows it's not luck, it's alignment.

What to Look For (Without Losing Your Mind)

If you're thinking, "Okay but I never see anything," let me gently drag you with love:

You might be looking for fireworks when your soul speaks in whispers.

Start here:

- Repeating numbers (111, 333, 555)

- Dreams you can't shake

- Songs that play at oddly perfect times

- Random overheard conversations that answer your question

- Feeling a sudden calm after making a hard decision

Pay attention to what pulls your attention.

That's not just coincidence. It's often energetic communication.

Science calls this cognitive resonance. Your body and intuition are attuned to truth, even before your brain makes sense of it.

SIGNS 101: How the Universe Slips Into Your DMs

If the Universe had social media, she wouldn't be posting thirst traps.

She'd be DMing you feathers, numbers, lyrics, and "coincidences" that are actually divine choreography.

1. Signs Are Personalized

Ask for one. Like, "If I'm meant to do this, show me a white fox."

And then chill. No obsessing. Curiosity invites; desperation blocks.

2. They're Not Always Loud

Sometimes it's a stranger saying the exact thing you were thinking.

Or a street name you keep seeing.

Or the same message popping up from different people.

3. They Show Up at Crossroads

- When you're breaking up
- Changing careers
- Moving cities
- Starting a new chapter

That's when signs come in hot. You're not being tested. You're being tuned.

4. The More You Trust, the Louder They Get

The universe speaks fluently in frequency.

When you stop gaslighting your gut, and start following that subtle "yes" or "no," more clarity lands.

5. When You Get a Sign:

- Pause.
- Acknowledge it.
- Say thank you.
- Ask, "What's next?"

Then listen with your whole body.

When You Feel Forgotten

You're not.

But if it feels like you've been left on spiritual read, run a quick self-check:

- Have you been asking for signs but ignoring them when they come?

- Have you been waiting for certainty instead of taking the first step?

- Have you been calling it confusion... but deep down, already know the answer?

You don't get a burning bush if you haven't even lit the match.

Let me tell you a little secret I've learned.

You don't have to sit on a mountain top or chant for 12 hours to manifest a life that lights your soul on fire. You do, however, need to get intentional with your energy. Here are seven small but mighty quantum-inspired rituals that rewired my mindset, aligned my frequency, and genuinely changed my life from the inside out.

1. Program your water with intention.

Every time I poured a glass of water, I started blessing it with a little wish. I'd whisper, "This water aligns me with my highest self." That's it. I know it sounds wild, but when you charge your daily rituals with intention, your energy shifts—and the results speak for themselves.

2. Use doorways as portals.

I began treating every doorway like a threshold into a new version of myself. I'd think, "I'm stepping into the timeline where everything I want already exists." It's subtle. It's powerful. It rewires your brain to expect good things.

3. Thank the universe in advance.

Instead of waiting for the miracle to land, I started showing gratitude like it already had. I'd say, "Thank you for the opportunities, the healing, the success," before anything had even happened. When your emotions catch up to the vision, reality has no choice but to match your energy.

4. Mirror pep talks (yes, seriously).

Every morning, I'd look in the mirror and remind myself: "You are powerful. Everything you desire is already on its way." Sounds cheesy. Works like magic. And honestly? We could all use a hype queen in our reflection.

5. Visualize before bed.

Right before sleep, I'd imagine my dream life like I was already living it. Not just the picture—but the feelings, the conversations, the smell of my future kitchen, the freedom, the peace. It helped my subconscious get on board with the future I was building.

6. Journal like it already happened.

Instead of writing down goals as "someday," I started writing entries from the perspective of already having them. "I'm so grateful for the new home, the aligned clients, the energy I wake up with." Writing it out tricks the brain, and your frequency follows.

7. Turn showers into energy resets.

Every shower became a sacred little ceremony. I'd imagine the water washing away fear, doubt, and anything that wasn't serving me. I'd say: "I release what's no longer aligned and make space for my desires." It turned a basic hygiene habit into a spiritual detox.

These aren't hacks. They're energetic declarations.

Small, sacred moments where I remembered who the hell I was.

And guess what?

It worked.

A Little Cheeky Truth

If I had received everything I begged for in 2019...

I'd be married to someone I no longer align with,

Living a "Pinterest-worthy" life that made my soul shrink.

What I thought was punishment?

Was protection.

What I thought was stagnation?

Was spiritual scaffolding.

What felt like failure?

Was redirection.

Now I look at my life, my peace, my partner, my path, and think:

No wonder she took her time.

Final Note (Divinely Timed, Of Course)

You're not behind.

You're just on divine timing.

Even if it's quiet.

Even if it's weird.

Even if you're googling angel numbers while crying into oat milk ice cream.

The Universe sees you.

She's not ghosting you, she's just moving mountains you haven't even seen yet.

So light the candle.

Ask the question.

And when the sign shows up, don't doubt it because it wasn't loud.

Your soul doesn't need noise to hear the truth.

It just needs you to pay attention.

No BS Reinvention Reflection: This isn't "woo-woo." This is truth. Tune in

Take what resonates, leave what doesn't, but don't ignore the signs.

Don't silence your gut.

Don't write off what makes your soul feel known.

1. What's one sign, number, or moment that's stuck with you, even if you didn't understand it at the time? Could it have been your soul nudging you?

   _____

   _____

   _____

   _____

   _____

   _____

2. What's one moment in your life you thought was a setback, but now realize it was divine redirection?

   _____

   _____

   _____

   _____

   _____

   _____

3. Who would you become if you truly believed everything happening right now is part of your awakening, not your punishment?

_____

_____

_____

_____

_____

_____

Remember.

The universe isn't punishing you.

She's preparing you.

Your breakdown isn't a dead end; it's a door.

Your delays aren't rejection; they're alignment.

And your signs?

They're not coincidences.

They're confirmations that you are exactly where you're meant to be, becoming who you were born to become.

Keep going.

She's not ghosting you.

She's guiding you home.

Affirmation to take with me:

I release the timeline. I trust the
process. What's mine cannot miss
me, even if it's taking the
scenic route.

PART THREE: THE REBIRTH

Chapter 13
From Wounded to Weaponized
(In the Best Way!)

So, you've been through some sh*t.

But that's not the shame—that's the superpower.

Spring 2025, my 10-year-old sat in the back seat of our SUV, tears quietly rolling down her cheeks.

She was supposed to walk into her jiu-jitsu class. She was dressed, hair tied up, bag packed. But today, she couldn't.

Not because she was tired.

Not because she didn't want to go.

But because the weight of the world was sitting on her tiny shoulders, and it had nothing to do with push-ups or sparring.

"They're going to think I'm fat... or ugly," she whispered.

That moment... still haunts me.

Not in the way that makes you collapse.

But in the way that makes you want to fight the entire system that taught your daughter to measure her worth by her body, before she's even old enough to fully understand what a "body image" is.

I turned around and looked at her. Her face flushed with emotion, her eyes glossy, her little hands gripping the seatbelt like it was holding her together.

And then she said something that floored me.

"You don't understand... you're perfect."

And right there, I felt this ripple, past me, future her, generations of women between us.

She couldn't see that I had once been her.

The Mirror in the Backseat

I took a deep breath and looked her in the eyes.

"No, baby. You don't even know how wildly perfect you are."

And then I told her the truth. Not the perfect mom version. Not the filtered, watered-down kind.

The real truth. The kind of truth I wish someone had spoken to me when I was her age.

I told her that I was bullied too.

For my ears.

For my teeth.

For being too skinny.

For being too quiet in some rooms and too loud in others.

For not fitting in. For trying too hard to.

And then I told her the story I hadn't shared in a long time, the one that still made me flinch a little, even all these years later.

I was in the 6th grade when a boy, my very first crush, looked at me and said:

"You have buck teeth. And your ears stick out like Dumbo. It's so ugly."

That moment tattooed itself on my brain.

I laughed it off like it didn't sting, but it did.

It stung in a way that words sometimes do when they come from someone you were hoping would like you.

After that, I never wore my hair up again.

I'd slick it down, tuck it behind my cheeks, use headbands, clips, try to tape them to my head, anything to keep those ears covered.

Not just for a year.

Not for junior high.

But for over a decade.

I was 24 years old, with a baby on my hip, before I wore my hair up in public without panicking.

Let that sink in.

I spent the majority of my life going to extremes not to show my ears.

I quit cheerleading because I would have to wear my hair up at competitions.

I wore headbands if I wanted to wear a ponytail.

I told my first boyfriend not to put my hair behind my ears when he was doing it to be lovely and romantic, and I said it "tickled too much."

I tried to crazy glue my ears to my head.

I even tried a hot glue gun and burnt the skin on the back of my head.

It took growing an entire human being and birthing a child to finally believe I was allowed to show my ears.

For some reason, having a child helps the level of "f***s given" lower drastically.

That's the level of quiet pain so many of us walk with, the kind we don't even know we're still carrying until someone (like our daughter) reflects it back to us.

Body Image Isn't Born, It's Modeled

Research from the National Eating Disorders Association shows that body dissatisfaction begins as early as age 5.

Children adopt our language about weight, food, and appearance, whether we mean to pass it on or not.

Kids don't just listen to what we say about them...

They absorb what we say about ourselves.

So when I see my daughter ache under the invisible pressure to be "perfect," I don't just see her pain, I see the ghosts of everything I once swallowed whole.

And I realize: I can't just break the cycle for her. I have to break it through me.

Maybe your wound wasn't your ears.

Maybe it was your weight.

Your skin.

Your voice.

Your laugh.

Your grades.

Your silence.

But I'd bet money there's a moment, buried somewhere, that made you change yourself to be more acceptable.

And you've been unpacking it ever since.

And that's the thing about shame.

It doesn't just visit... it builds a home inside of you.

Until one day, you knock on the door...

And finally tell it to get the hell out.

The Inherited Pain We Never Meant to Pass Down

Here's what I've learned as a mother, a woman, and a lifelong healing-in-progress human:

Our unhealed wounds don't stay quiet forever.

They show up in the people we love.

They repeat themselves through what we normalize.

They echo in moments we never expected, like a jiu-jitsu parking lot on a Thursday night.

We don't just inherit our mother's eyes or our father's stubbornness.

We inherit their survival tactics.

Their fear of being seen.

Their generational "don't cry" conditioning.

Their patterns of pleasing, perfectionism,
shrinking, enduring.

And unless we pause...

Unless we really pause and ask, "Is this mine or did I
inherit this?"

We keep the cycle spinning.

But Every Now and Then... We Get a Sacred Interruption

A child breaks down.

A mirror reflects something too familiar.

A quiet moment becomes a spotlight.

And that's our invitation.

The nervous system works like a thermostat. It adjusts
to whatever "normal" was in our early years.

So if our normal was emotional suppression, shame, or
conditional love?

That's what our body calibrates to... until we decide to

rewire it.

According to neuroscience, the amygdala, the brain's fear center, responds rapidly to perceived threats, including social rejection or shame.

But with repeated safety and new experiences, we can teach the brain that vulnerability isn't dangerous. It's a bridge to connection.

Integration begins with noticing the discomfort.

Interrupting the loop.

And rewriting the story, not just for ourselves, but for the generation that follows.

The Shame We Don't Talk About

Okay, it's shame's turn in the hot seat.

Not the 'oops I sent a risky text' shame.

The gut-wrenching, throat-tightening, "If anyone knew this about me, they'd leave" kind of shame.

We all have it.

And we all think we're the only one carrying it.

Shame says: "You're not enough."

Shame says: "You're too much."

Shame says: "Stay small and maybe no one will notice you're faking it."

We don't talk about it because we think it makes us unworthy.

But the truth is: Your shame is the seed of your transformation.

Not because you deserved the pain.

But because you survived it.

> Brené Brown defines shame as the fear of disconnection, that something we've done or experienced makes us unworthy of love and belonging.

But she also says shame cannot survive being spoken out loud.

Every time we name it, we shrink it.

Every time we own it, we reclaim ourselves.

From Story to Strength

When I told my daughter I'd find a photo of myself at her age, it wasn't a throwaway comment.

I wanted her to see it.

To see that I wasn't born the woman I am now.

To see the braces, the awkward hair, the outfit that didn't quite fit right.

To see the little girl who tried so hard to be liked.

Because sometimes the best way to help someone love themselves... is to show them the version of you who didn't.

We live in a world obsessed with the "after."

But sometimes the evolution happens in the middle photo, the one we're too afraid to show.

That's the one with the miracle.

You Are Allowed to Talk About the Pain, Before It's Pretty

We think we have to wait to "get through it" before we can share our story.

But that's a lie we tell ourselves to avoid vulnerability.

Your voice doesn't need a polished ending to be powerful.

You don't need a Ted Talk version of your healing to speak truth.

Sometimes, what heals someone else is hearing your truth while it's still messy.

While it still trembles when you say it.

While you're still figuring it out.

"You can't lead from a wound, but you can lead from a scar."

And scars mean you didn't stay down.

Weaponized, Not Wounded

This chapter isn't about pretending you're okay.

It's about understanding that your pain didn't destroy you; it designed you.

Your wounds weren't weaknesses.

They were wake-up calls.

They didn't happen to you.

They happened for the version of you you're shifting into.

You are not too complicated to be loved.

You are not too damaged to lead.

You are weaponized.

In the best way.

The Sacred Power of Storytelling

When you share your story, the real one, not the sanitized one, you do two things:

1. You take your power back.

2. You light the way for someone else.

Every time you speak the truth of what you've lived through, shame loses its grip.

And someone else finds the courage to keep going.

So no, your story isn't "too much."

It's just enough to set someone else free.

Let's Part For Now With This:

Your wounds were not your weakness.

They were your weapons in disguise.

You didn't just get through,

You grew through.

And now?

You get to be the woman who turns mirrors into windows,

So every little girl who comes after you sees what's possible,

Because you chose to heal out loud.

No BS Reinvention Reflection: This isn't a throwaway moment. This is the part where the story starts to change, because you finally decide to own it. Not hide it. Not downplay it. Not dress it up to make other people comfortable. Your past doesn't need a filter; it needs a voice. And that voice? It's yours now.

1. What part of your story have you been afraid to own and why?

   _____

   _____

   _____

   _____

   _____

2. Write your "I made it through" statement. Make it raw. Make it bold. Make it yours.
   (i.e. I made it through silence. I made it through shame. I made it through being underestimated.)

   _____

   _____

   _____

   _____

   _____

3. What have you survived that could help someone else feel less alone?

_____

_____

_____

_____

_____

Meet her.

Buck teeth, big ears, questionable fashion choices...

and a heart that just wanted to be liked.

She had no idea she'd grow up to become a woman who writes books, sets boundaries, and heals bloodlines.

But she always had it in her.

This is where it started.

If I could go back and tell her anything, I'd say:

"One day, your mess will become your magic.

You're not too much. You're just early."

And honestly?

She'd probably still try to hide her ears, but now? I'd help her tie her ponytail higher.

Chapter 14
Plot Twist: This Is Just Your Warm-Up Round

The Spark I Didn't See Coming

I was lying in bed with Brad in spring 2024, and let's be honest, it was late for us. I'm talking 8:30 p.m., the kind of wild Friday night only parents of young kids can appreciate. Hockey was on, so naturally, he was fired up. Meanwhile, I was deep in my usual scroll-hole when our conversation took an unexpected turn.

We were chatting about his private lending profile. He was strategizing ways to cut costs, weighing the pros and cons of becoming a mortgage broker himself to eliminate the middleman.

And then I casually blurted it out:

"Well… what does it take to become a mortgage broker? Maybe I could become your middleman?"

He looked at me and smiled. I smiled back. We both knew I was more of a science girl with a marketing brain. Math? Not exactly my claim to fame... unless we're talking girl math, which I proudly consider a superpower.

But in that exact moment, something clicked.

I felt it. A buzz through my arms and legs. A spark. A whisper in my gut that said:

"Wait... what's here?"

The Google Spiral That Changed Everything

We went down a rabbit hole together. Full-on tag team typing:

"How to become a mortgage broker in Ontario."

I had no idea what I was doing.

I didn't know what schooling it required.

I didn't know how long it would take.

I didn't know if I'd even like it.

But I was hooked.

I stayed up way too late that night, elbows-deep in research. Scanning Reddit threads, watching YouTube videos, reading government licensing info like it was juicy gossip. The more I learned, the more intrigued I became.

And somewhere between "how long does the exam

take" and "mortgage broker memes," I started to feel it:

Could this be my way out of dental hygiene?

Could this be the thing that gets me home with my kids again, without burning out in the process?

Could this be... my next best adventure?

Three days later, I walked up to Brad like a woman possessed and said:

"I'm in. Let's do this."

And if you know me, you know:

I didn't just "dip a toe." I dove in headfirst, high ponytail flying.

I Didn't Know the Math... But I Knew the Energy

Let's be clear: I wasn't some mortgage prodigy. I knew absolutely nothing about GDS, TDS, LTV, or why fixed rates were having their own hot girl summer.

But I did know the energy didn't lie.

You know that electric-feeling-in-your-body vibe that shows up when something's meant for you? That's not caffeine. That's alignment.

According to neuroscience, when we feel emotionally charged by something new, a bold idea, a career pivot, a big dream, our brain releases dopamine, the "motivation molecule." That buzz you feel?

That's your body saying, "This could be life-changing. Keep going."

So I did.

Because I've learned to trust those tingles.

The quiet nudges.

The sparks that don't go away after a few days.

That's not distraction. That's direction.

And if something lights you up and keeps calling you back?

That's your green light. Even if it doesn't make sense yet.

When Life Forced My Hand

Here's the part I didn't plan:

My daughter, Amelia, was struggling.

Our youngest had been recently diagnosed with autism, and although she was doing her best, school was a battlefield. I would get calls, sometimes tearful voicemails, while I was still wearing my scrubs, standing in a sterilization room trying to pretend everything was fine.

She'd be in full panic mode, begging me to come

home. The sound of her voice on those calls still breaks my heart.

I'd excuse myself between patients, hands trembling in the bathroom, feeling helpless.

Feeling like a mom divided down the middle.

I knew in my bones I couldn't keep living like that.

Clocking in while my daughter's world was falling apart? No.

Trying to numb my own internal wiring so I could survive the day? No.

I needed a career that let me breathe again, and one that let her know I was there when she needed me.

Mortgage brokering wasn't just a pivot. It was a lifeline.

To her.

To me.

To our entire family.

The truth? As a hygienist, I spent years holding a tiny mirror, working upside down in someone's mouth, all while my Spotify playlist blared in the background like a chaotic soundtrack to my slow mental unraveling.
I didn't just want out, I needed out. It was time for something else, and I was all in.

The Pivot That Gave Me Everything I Never Knew I Wanted

Becoming a mortgage agent wasn't just a career move.

It was a reclamation.

It gave me flexibility, the kind that lets us take off to the lake on a Tuesday with the girls, just because the sun is out and the snacks are packed.

It gave me the opportunity to work toward financial independence, a path where I didn't have to wait for a raise or beg for time off to live my life.

It gave me the space to be the parent and partner I wanted to be, not the one who lost her "edge."

It gave me the freedom to grow, to return to the wild, creative, entrepreneurial version of me that had been hiding behind the charade that scrub life was the life for her.

It gave me my spark back.

I no longer came home drained to the bone, pouring from an empty cup. I worked from home lit up, knowing that my work was changing lives.

And most of all...

It gave me purpose again.

Now I get to help people.

I get to build something that's mine.

And this time, I get to do it my way.

Who would've thought?

Sure as hell not me.

But that's the cool part about reinvention:

It rarely shows up wrapped in a perfect little bow.

Sometimes, it sneaks in during a random hockey night conversation... and changes everything.

The Client Who Cracked My Heart Wide Open (A Story I'll Never Forget)

I'll never forget one of my first mortgage clients.

I triple-checked every number. I memorized policies like they were Shakespeare. My hand shook pressing "send" on the email to underwriting.

I wasn't fast. But I was thorough.

I wasn't flashy. But I cared.

This client wasn't just a file. She was a mom of three who had been told, "You probably won't qualify," by someone else.

But guess what?

She did qualify.

And when I called her with the approval, I teared up, big time.

She cried.

Her kids screamed in the background.

It hit me like a freight train:

This is what I was meant to do.

And I'll be honest... when she messaged me after, saying,

"I finally feel excited about life again,"

I knew this job was different.

This wasn't just number crunching. This was autonomic system work. This was advocacy. This was empowerment with a signature line.

The Psychology of Reinvention (Let's Get Nerdy Again)

According to neuroscientist Dr. Andrew Huberman, the brain resists change because it activates the amygdala, the fear center. It's your internal alarm bell, wired for survival, not innovation.

It's not that you're doing something wrong.

It's that your brain is doing exactly what it was built to do: keep you safe.

But the kicker?

Your brain doesn't distinguish between real danger and emotional discomfort. That awkward first networking call? That career change? That Instagram post announcing a new title?

Your brain reads all of it as risk.

But every time you take a small, courageous action toward the future version of you, you create new neural pathways.

That's neuroplasticity. And that's your superpower.

So when your hands shake? That's normal.

When your inner voice whispers, "What are you doing?" That's normal.

When you want to go back to comfort just to breathe?
Also normal.

Growth isn't the absence of fear.

It's the decision to keep going, with shaky hands but
steady vision.

The Future Self Who Led Me Here

Now that I look back, I realize it wasn't just some fluke
idea that got me here.

It was my future self guiding the way.

She knew what I didn't yet:

That I was built for more.

That I was worthy of ease, alignment, abundance.

That I didn't have to earn rest or prove worthiness
through suffering.

And you know what?

She's still leading.

I picture her often, sitting in her sunlit office, sipping
coffee, helping families get into homes they thought
were out of reach.

She smiles and says,

"Keep going. We're just getting started."

The Words That Shifted Everything

Not long after that, I saw a post on Instagram that pierced me right in the chest. It said:

"Show me how good it can get."

Simple. But something in it cracked me open.

It reminded me that I didn't need to wait until I was struggling to ask for help... or until I was burned out to deserve better.

I was allowed to want more, more alignment, more joy, more holy-sht-this-is-my-life* moments.

I realized I didn't want just fine anymore.

I wanted extraordinary.

Not because I was greedy, but because I was finally ready to believe I was worthy of it.

Now I say it all the time, when I start my day, before a call, when I'm about to send an offer, or even just when I tuck my kids in with a full heart:

"Show me how good it can get."

It's not a demand.

It's a declaration.

One that reminds me I'm not here to settle.

I'm here to be blown away.

And every time I ask, the Universe answers, in ways I never could've scripted.

You don't have to know exactly who you're becoming to begin.

You just have to feel the flicker...

...and trust it enough to light the match.

Then let the fire show you who you've been all along.

So Let Me Leave You With This...

This year has been one for the books.

Not just because of the certifications or the checkmarks.

But because I met myself again.

I rebuilt.

I reimagined.

I remembered.

It's been a series of lessons, of hard truths, of wild pivots and beautiful messes. I've been humbled. I've been cracked open. I've cried into my keyboard and belly-laughed over coffee.

I've asked, "Who am I now?" more times than I can count.

But here's what I've learned:

You don't have to know exactly who you're blossoming into to start.

You just have to trust the spark, and follow it with your whole damn heart.

So whatever you're dreaming of...

Even if it seems ridiculous.

Even if it's outside your degree, your comfort zone, your friend group, or your former identity...

Do it anyway.

Because the most exciting, fulfilling, badass chapters of your life?

Are almost always the ones that start with:

"Wait... what if I actually did this?"

When the Old You Fights to Stay

When you're unfolding into someone new, your old self doesn't just disappear.

You've envisioned the life you want.

You've started showing up like her.

You've said the affirmations, done the work, made the shift...

But then,

That old voice creeps in.

You start overthinking.

You scroll for validation.

You replay memories from when you didn't believe in yourself yet.

This isn't failure.

It's just the past version of you trying to survive one more round.

It doesn't fade quietly.

It speaks in hesitation.

In self-doubt.

In all the ways you used to keep yourself small.

It'll whisper:

"Be careful."

"Don't get too excited."

"See? Nothing's changed."

But it's not the world rejecting you.

It's your old conditioning trying to pull you back into the comfort zone.

The one where fear still runs the show.

And if you're not aware, you'll believe it.

You'll react.

You'll spiral.

You'll forget you've evolved.

And you'll slide back into patterns you've already outgrown.

So What Do You Do?

You don't fight it.

You notice it.

You feel it without letting it drive.

And then you remind yourself:

"That's not me anymore.

That's just a reflex.

A memory.

A version of me that no longer gets to lead."

Then you choose again.

You come back to the version of you who's already living the life you want.

The one who knows they're worthy, supported, and already becoming.

OLD YOU THOUGHT...	NEW YOU KNOWS...
This is the end of the road.	This is just the starting line... again.
I have to stay in what I trained for.	Your passion > your diploma. Always.
But I'm not qualified.	If it excites you, you'll figure it out.
I should stay safe and stable.	I'm allowed to choose freedom and fulfillment.
What if I fail?	What if I *fly*?
I can't pivot now.	Pivoting is the path. Not the problem.
It's too late to start over.	Reinvention doesn't care about your age or resume.
This doesn't make logical sense.	Energy doesn't lie. Follow the spark.
I'm scared to leave what's familiar.	Familiar ≠ fulfilling
What if people don't get it?	The people meant for me will *feel* it. The rest? Bye.

No BS Reinvention Reflection: Because sometimes the biggest plot twist isn't life changing—it's you deciding to finally bet on yourself.

1. What decision have you been putting off because it feels unfamiliar or "not you?" Could it actually be your next breakthrough?

   _____

   _____

   _____

   _____

2. Where are you still playing small out of fear of the unknown, and what would it look like to leap anyway?

   _____

   _____

   _____

   _____

3. What's one thing that's been quietly exciting you? (Spoiler: That's your soul speaking. Go there.)

   _____

   _____

   _____

   _____

Zoom Out for a Sec

If you had zero fear. What would feel
most exciting right now? This is your
fastest path. Every time.
Don't negotiate with your intuition.
That spark you feel isn't random.

Chapter 15
Your Future Self Called, She Wants You to Start Acting Like Her (Identity Shift)

"Stop being an extra in your own movie. You only get one script, step into the role you were born to play." — The Main Character Theory

She's got boundaries, glowing skin, and peace in her group chats.

Your future self? She's thriving.

And she's wondering what the hell you're waiting for.

There comes a moment in every woman's life when she realizes: Oh... I've outgrown this version of me.

Not in an explosive, toss-your-life-into-the-fire way (although hey, sometimes we do that too).

But in the quiet knowing kind of way, the kind where your old habits start to itch, your old circle starts to feel noisy, and your old excuses stop sounding like you.

Your future self doesn't arrive in a package.

She's built, habit by habit.

Decision by decision.

Boundary by boundary.

And if you listen closely... you'll hear her.

Not in the "you should be doing more" guilt-trip kind of way,

But in the fiery whisper kind of way that says:

"You're not lost. You're just in between versions."

What an Identity Shift Actually Means

An identity shift isn't about faking it until you make it.

It's about remembering who the hell you are under all the conditioning.

It's not about buying the $80 moon-charged crystal water bottle (although, cute).

It's about making aligned, repeated, embodied decisions based on who you say you're expanding as.

This isn't a makeover.

It's a return.

To the you who's always been there, under the people-pleasing, trauma patterns, TikTok scroll-holes, and the neutral beige throw pillows you didn't even like but bought because YouTube told you to.

Here's What Identity Shifting Sounds Like in Real Life:

- "I don't chase, I choose."

- "No, thank you. That's not aligned with the woman I'm becoming."

- "I used to say yes to keep the peace. Now I say no to protect mine."

- "That old me? I love her. But she doesn't get to run the show anymore."

This is the voice of your future self stepping in, interrupting the inner saboteur that's been narrating your life for way too long.

NEUROPLASTICITY

Psychologists call this process self-directed neuroplasticity. Which is a fancy way of saying: when you change your language, you change your brain. When you upgrade your self-concept, you literally rewire your default settings.

Let's Talk Future You

She's not spotless.

She still gets puffy eyes and second-guesses herself sometimes.

But she knows her worth.

She doesn't argue with people who are committed to misunderstanding her.

She makes money moves without waiting for permission.

She wears what she wants.

She says what needs to be said.

She doesn't beg, chase, or shrink.

She doesn't text back at 10 p.m. when she's drained.

She doesn't overexplain her boundaries.

And she sure as hell doesn't settle for someone who says, "You're too much."

Because now she knows:

Too much for them = just right for herself.

The people living the life you dream about aren't necessarily more talented, smarter, or better than you. They're just the ones who decided to stop sitting in the background, waiting for permission. They stepped onto the stage, claimed the spotlight, and refused to give up when things got hard.

This is what I mean when I talk about embodying your future self. You don't wait until you've "earned it" or until the timing feels perfect. You decide you're the main character now, not the supporting role, not the understudy. And when you start living like that, everything shifts.

But Old You Wants to Keep It Safe

Old you isn't evil.

She's just wired for survival.

She's the one who:

- People-pleased to avoid conflict
- Said yes when she wanted to scream no
- Dated the guy who "had potential" and ignored the red flags
- Tolerated toxic group chats, undercharging, and silent resentment

She meant well. She got you this far.

But she was operating from fear, not embodiment.

So now?

We honor her, and retire her.

Fun fact: your brain hates change. It loves routine and certainty, even if it's miserable. That's why identity shifts can feel so clunky at first. You're not just changing habits. You're breaking neurological autopilot.

Future You Energy, Let's Break It Down

Want to step into your future self?

Cool. But we're not just thinking about her. We're acting like her.

Here's what that looks like:

1. **Language Shift**

How you speak is how you think.

And how you think is how you show up.

- Old You: "I hope this works out."
  Future You: "It's already mine. I'm just aligning with it."

- Old You: "I'm not sure I'm ready."
  Future You: "I'll figure it out when I get there."

- Old You: "Sorry for the delay."
  Future You: "Thanks for your patience."

Language shift = life shift.

Start talking like she's already here.

2. Style Shift

This isn't about trends.

It's about embodied energy.

Wear the clothes that make you walk differently.

Choose outfits that make you feel like you've arrived.

Not for others, for your own damn reflection.

Power doesn't come from the blazer.

It comes from the woman wearing it like armor.

> Neuroscience shows that "enclothed cognition," what we wear, directly influences how we behave and feel about ourselves. So yes. The vibe check starts in your closet.

3. Money Shift

Future You checks her bank account without spiraling.

She doesn't make decisions from panic or guilt.

She invests in her growth.

She stops saying, "I can't afford that," and starts saying:

"It's not a priority right now... but it will be."

That's financial self-respect.

Money is just energy in numbers form.

The more you honor your current reality while envisioning where you're headed, the faster they align.

4. Relationship Shift

She doesn't chase people who make her question her worth.

She doesn't perform for love.

She doesn't keep explaining her needs to people who refuse to hear her.

She dates, and befriends, with standards, not scarcity.

And she's not afraid to outgrow a room if it means growing into herself.

5. Energy Shift

She protects her peace like a paid security guard.

- She unfollows with ease.

- She leaves unread if her nervous system says "no."

- She doesn't attend every argument she's invited to.

"I'm not available for chaos anymore." That's her love language.

And your nervous system?

It thanks you every time you choose calm over chaos.

I Knew I Was Her When...

I once got a message from someone I used to bend over backwards for.

Old me would've jumped. Replied at 10 p.m. Said " of course."

But this time, I paused. I checked in.

And I said:

"Hey love, I'm offline this week, hope everything's okay."

I didn't explain. I didn't spiral.

That's when I knew: She's here. I'm her.

I knew I was her when I:

- Planned my weekends around people who fueled me, not drained me.

- Turned down an old friend's wedding invite because being around my past self wasn't worth shrinking my current one.

- Spoke my truth calmly instead of biting my tongue for peace.

- Complimented my reflection instead of critiquing it.

- Let love in, even when my brain said, "Protect yourself," but my body whispered, "Trust this."

And when I knelt instead of snapped at my daughters,

offering presence instead of punishment,

I knew,

She wasn't a fantasy.

She was already here.

A Note on the Mind-Body Piece

Embodiment doesn't just happen in your mindset.

It shows up in your body's alarm system.

You may know who you're emerging as,

But if your body is still regulated by old fears,

Your actions will default to safety, even when they don't serve you.

That's why this shift takes practice.

Try this:

- Speak her thoughts out loud

- Journal as if you're her now

- Make one "brave" decision per week

- Move like her. Breathe like her. Eat like her. Set boundaries like her.

Eventually, your brain rewires.

Eventually, your body catches up.

Eventually, you stop trying... because you are.

Fire Quote Break

> "You don't attract what you want.
> You attract what you embody."

Read that again.

You can want peace, love, overflow, success,

But if you're embodying scarcity, overgiving, resentment, and self-doubt?

That's the signal you're sending.

And energy doesn't lie.

Your future self isn't manifesting a new life.

She's living it, one aligned, uncomfortable, powerful choice at a time.

Future Me Language: Identity Upgrade in Action

Old Me Said...	Future Me Says...
Sorry for being annoying!	Thanks for your patience.
I hope I'm not too much.	I'm not for everyone, and that's my superpower.
I don't want to make a big deal.	This matters to me, so I'm speaking up.
I'm probably overthinking it.	My intuition is valid.
I'm not good at that.	I'm learning and getting better every day.
I don't know if I can.	I'll rise to meet it, like I always do.
It's fine, don't worry about me.	I deserve support too.

You Become Who You Identify As, Period.

You don't become what you hope for.

You become what you identify as.

Your identity creates your reality.

Your words reinforce your identity.

Your repeated choices lock it in.

If you keep saying, "I'm always overwhelmed,"

Guess what? You'll keep living in chaos.

If you say, "I'm terrible with money,"

Your brain will block opportunities to learn how to manage it.

If you say, "I'm not that kind of person..."

You're literally reinforcing your limits.

But the good news?

You can flip that script.

You can rewrite your self-concept in real time.

Try these swaps:

- "I'm working on becoming someone who protects their energy."

- "I choose peace over people-pleasing now."

- "I may not be there yet, but this is who I'm becoming."

- "I'm the kind of woman who follows through."

- "I'm learning to trust myself more every day."

Your words are not just habits.

They are programming.

And every time you speak with intention, you reinforce who you are becoming instead of who you've been trying to outgrow.

So next time you say, "I'm just someone who..."

Finish that sentence like your future self is listening.

Because she is.

And she's not waiting.

She's already moving.

She's already unfolding.

Let's Part With This:

When you're becoming someone new, your old self doesn't just disappear.

You've envisioned the life you want.

You've started showing up like her.

You've said the affirmations, done the work, made the shift...

But then,

That old voice creeps in.

You start overthinking.

You scroll for validation.

You replay memories from when you didn't believe in yourself yet.

This isn't failure.

It's just the past version of you trying to survive one more round.

It doesn't fade quietly.

It speaks in hesitation.

In self-doubt.

In all the ways you used to keep yourself small.

It'll whisper:

"Be careful."

"Don't get too excited."

"See? Nothing's changed."

But it's not the world rejecting you.

It's your old conditioning trying to pull you back into the comfort zone.

The one where fear still runs the show.

And if you're not aware, you'll believe it.

You'll react.

You'll spiral.

You'll forget you've evolved.

And you'll slide back into patterns you've already outgrown.

So what do you do?

You don't fight it.

You notice it.

You feel it without letting it drive.

And then you remind yourself:

"That's not me anymore.

That's just a reflex.

A memory.

A version of me that no longer gets to lead."

Then you choose again.

You come back to the version of you who's already living the life you want.

The one who knows they're worthy, supported, and already becoming.

The After: Love, Lessons & a Life We're Still Building

You've been here for the turmoil.

You've walked with me through the collapse, the identity deaths, the panic spirals, the decisions that made no sense to anyone but my higher self. You've seen me rage cry, upgrade, backslide, and come back swinging, stronger, softer, louder, and finally... real.

So, it only feels right to show you what came after.

Not the filtered, "she found her forever love" kind of ending.

Not the curated dream with the matching mugs and affirmations in gold foil.

I'm talking about the real after.

The one no one posts on social media.

The part that's dreamy and exhausting. Sacred and messy. Healing and hilarious.

The part when the hard work actually begins, but this time, you're not doing it alone.

This part right here? It's the good stuff.

After I left my marriage, with nothing but my basics, two daughters, and a wild amount of self-respect, I didn't just rebuild my life. I rebuilt my definition of home. Brad and I bought a house together. Not a fairytale palace. A real, intentionally chosen home. One where we both arrived not as saviors, but as partners, carrying our own pasts, the girls, our wounds, and a willingness to do things differently. He sold one of his rental properties, I got bought out of my marital home, and we signed onto an entirely new chapter. Only weeks later, in a symbolic moment of full-circle, *OMG is this really happening*, we sold my old rusted Nissan Rogue (may she rest in crusty, clunky peace) and bought a white BMW, the kind of car my younger self would've looked at and thought, "Whoa. She must have her s*** together."*

(Spoiler: I still do not have my s*** entirely together, but the car has air-conditioned seats and sometimes that's enough.)

And no, we aren't married yet. (I know you're all wondering!)

It's something we talk about. I joke and send him rings monthly. Hint hint.

We laugh about it, because we love this season of our life.

We don't feel like a wedding or a certificate is what validates who we are or the love we've built.

One day we'll probably tie the knot (mainly so I can stop calling him "boyfriend" or "partner Brad," like I'm introducing a contestant on a couples' game show).

But until then? We're in no rush.

Because what we've got is already solid. Already sacred. Already ours.

And honestly... if you can survive permanent sleep regressions, summer break with the kids home 24/7, and trying to agree on a thermostat setting, you're basically married.

But the real flex?

Isn't the car. Or the house. Or even the "we made it" vibes. It's what happens inside that house.

We live in a whirlwind of love, learning, appointments, routines, reminders, and "Wait, did anyone feed the dogs today?"

We parent two neurospicy little girls, one of whom is on the autism spectrum. They're both fierce, sensitive, wildly intelligent, and emotionally tuned-in, and raising them is the single most sacred, stretching, gut-punching and heart-bursting thing we've ever done.

We also co-parent on a 50/50 schedule. Our homes are wildly different, and that's okay. The kids get something unique from each space, and somehow, we make it all work. We communicate often. Brad and their dad get along well; they've even done work together. We've shared dinners at his place, just the five of us, choosing mutual respect over ego. Our youngest tends to struggle more with transitions, so she stays with us a little more often, or sometimes, we send one of the dogs to his house so she still feels that sense of safety and consistency. We talk openly with the girls about our setup. We answer their questions honestly, give them space to feel it all, and remind them that it's okay to love everyone in different ways, and there's no competition in a home built on love. We struggle, of course. It's not flawless. But we move forward. Because there's no room in our home for resentment, jealousy, or old stories. Only oneness.

There are many days that start with meltdowns before caffeine.

Days when we're tag-teaming therapy appointments, calming big feelings in the school parking lot, and re-explaining for the millionth time why scratchy tags are basically a hate crime.

There are school calls.

Sleepless nights.

Hiding in the pantry sessions.

Moments when I'm Googling "how to not ruin your children while also surviving motherhood."

Moments when Brad brings me tea, rubs my back, and tells me I'm doing a great job, even when I don't believe it.

Moments when I remind him that we're a team, even when the house looks like a tornado made of laundry and neurodivergent mayhem just blew through.

And still...

There's softness.

There's laughter.

There's the kind of love that doesn't require you to mask up, or be seamless, just present.

We don't always get it right.

We lose it sometimes.

We apologize.

We course-correct.

We meet in the kitchen at 7:42 p.m. and whisper "we're doing our best" while eating gluten free cereal over the sink.

And somehow, that feels like success.

Because I spent years in relationships that were rooted in performance, perfectionism, and people-pleasing, and now, I finally know what safe love feels like.

And damn, it's worth the rewiring.

Final No-BS Love Lessons (From This Season of Our Lives):

- Aligned love doesn't sweep you off your feet. It helps carry your bags while you climb.

- You don't have to be fully healed to be deeply loved. But you do have to be honest.

- If love makes you shrink, it's not love. It's survival mode in disguise.

- Real relationships aren't perfect. But they are safe. Consistent. Intentional.

- The "right person" won't complete you. They'll respect who you've become.

- Family isn't always DNA. Sometimes it's two imperfect people, raising neurodivergent kids, burning chicken nuggets, and healing generational wounds on a Tuesday night.

If you're reading this from your own messy middle...

If you're still unpacking the old stories...

Still wondering if clarity ever shows up after chaos...

Still hoping for a life that doesn't require you to abandon yourself to belong...

Let this be your reminder:

You can rewrite everything.

You can start again.

You can build the kind of love and family that doesn't ask you to perform, only to show up.

Love won't save you.

But the right love will sit beside you while you do your own saving.

And family? It might look nothing like you imagined.

But if it's built with presence, grace, and a little humor, it's already holy.

Sometimes, the fairytale isn't about being rescued.

It's about becoming the version of you who no longer needs to be.

This isn't the end of my story.

It's just where I stopped pretending I had to do it all alone.

And maybe, just maybe...

It's where yours begins.

No BS Reinvention Reflection: Because playing small was never part of the plan.

1. What's one sentence you say often that doesn't align with the woman you want to become? Rewrite it now. Make it something she would say. Then say it out loud. Daily. Until it sticks.

   _____

   _____

   _____

   _____

2. If your future self was watching you today... would she feel proud? Would she feel seen? Or would she wonder what the hell you're still waiting for?

   _____

   _____

   _____

   _____

3. Make a "Future Me Energy" list: How she talks. What she tolerates. What she wears. What she no longer entertains.

   _____

   _____

   _____

   _____

Let's part for now, but not before you promise to start showing up for YOU:

Remember, the universe doesn't hand things out to the most deserving; it co-creates with the most daring.

It doesn't respond to wishful thinking from your comfort zone. It responds to action. To bravery. To the woman who laces up her shoes, even with shaky hands and a messy past, and says, "Let's go."

God, Source, Life, whatever you call it, is not passive. It's a living, breathing force that flows with you, not for you. And when you move with clear intent and wild courage, the path clears. The signs align. The doors crack open. Not because you're lucky, but because you're finally in motion.

This isn't about hustling for your worth. It's about partnering with life. It's about trusting that your aligned, honest, heart-led action sends ripples into the quantum field. And that energy? That momentum? It always comes back.

The universe doesn't need you perfect. It needs you present.

So stop waiting to be ready. Show up. Messy. Human. Lit up by your own truth.

Because when you show up fully, life meets you there, and then some.

thank you

A Final Love Note From Me to You

Well look at you, turning the final page like the badass you are.

Thank you for being here. Truly.

For letting me into your heart, your headspace, and maybe even the messy parts you don't show anyone. It's been an honor to walk this journey with you.

My biggest hope? That you feel braver. Louder. Lighter. And a little more you than when you started.

That you saw yourself somewhere in these chapters and realized... Whoa, I'm stronger than I thought.

Now, if this book lit a fire under you, made you laugh, cry, or ugly-snort in public (bonus points), I'd love for you to help me spread the magic.

Sharing a quick review on Amazon or Goodreads is the easiest way to help more women find these words. And who knows? Your review could be the exact nudge someone else needs to stop playing small.

I'd also love to connect with you, for real.

Follow me on Instagram @jessica_spence88

Tag your fave quote.

Shoot me a message.

Invite me to your podcast.

Start a book club.

Send me a meme.

Let's keep this real, raw, and alive.

The book may be ending, but your reinvention is just getting started.

With a wild amount of love,

Jess

Your reinvention hype girl, always.

Afterword

If you've made it here, take a breath.

Not a shallow one, a deep, belly-filling, soul-softening kind.

Because... holy smokes, that took courage.

You didn't just flip pages, you faced yourself.

You called your own bluff.

You whispered truth to the parts of you that were exhausted from holding it all together with dry shampoo and optimism.

You sat with the mirror and didn't flinch.

And that? That's worth celebrating.

Maybe you're not skipping off into the sunset yet.

Maybe you're still piecing it all together with equal parts journal prompts and iced coffee.

Maybe you're still learning to rest without needing to "earn it."

All of that is okay. More than okay, it's real.

Rebuilding isn't a glow-up montage with a Rihanna soundtrack (although that'd be nice).

Reinvention is rarely tidy.

Sometimes, it looks like a mascara meltdown on your kitchen floor at 2 a.m.

Sometimes, it looks like saying "no" and then spiraling about it for 3 hours.

Sometimes, it's just putting on real pants and calling that a win.

So let this sink in:

You're not a self-help project.

You're a whole dang person.

Messy, radiant, funny, emotional, powerful, trying-your-best-on-a-Tuesday person.

You're not meant to do this seamlessly. You're meant to do it honestly.

So here's what I hope for you:

I hope you leave this book a little bolder.

A little louder.

A little less tolerant of BS, especially your own.

I hope you remember that your softness is not weakness, your boundaries are not rude, and your dreams are not inconvenient.

I hope you keep showing up for your life, even when it's awkward, even when it's uncomfortable, even when you'd rather watch 16 episodes of "New Girl" in a row.

Because if we're truthful,

You're already doing it.

You've already begun.

And no one gets to decide what your timeline looks like, not your mom, not society, not that one girl from high school who sells candles and subtle judgment on Facebook.

You're the main character now.

So take the leap.

Take the nap.

Take your power back.

And when the world asks, "Who does she think she is?"

Smile politely and say:

"I am the author, not the aftermath. And I rise every damn time I remember who the hell I am."

With grit, grace, and a whole lot of laughs,

Jessica

Acknowledgements

Writing this book was part therapy, part rebellion, and part divine intervention. I couldn't have done it without the village, both seen and unseen, that carried me through.

To my daughters, Isabella and Amelia: You are my greatest teachers and the reason I became unbreakable in the first place. Everything I do is for you. Thank you for your patience during "mama's writing days," and for reminding me what wonder looks like in its purest form.

To Brad, the love of my life: You showed me that safe love exists. Thank you for treating me and the girls like royalty, for encouraging my wildest dreams, and for knowing when I need creme brûlée... or silence.

To my soul clients, sisters, and every woman who ever messaged me with "I don't know who I am anymore": This book was written with you in mind. Your vulnerability lit the path for these pages. You're not alone, and you never were.

To my past self, the scared one, the messy one, the one who kept getting back up: Thank you. I'm proud of you.

To the universe (and probably ten thousand angel numbers): Thank you for the signs, the unravelling, the , and the occasional cosmic smack upside the head. I heard you.

To every woman who picks up this book, thank you for trusting me to walk beside you. I hope you walk away remembering who the hell you are.

With more love than I can type,

Jessica

About the Author

Jessica Spence is a certified spiritual life coach, speaker, and now Mortgage Agent, who went from 60 pounds overweight, daily panic attacks, and leaving a toxic marriage with her babies and the basics... to building multiple businesses, a bold new identity, and a beautiful life with a man who treats her and her daughters like queens.

A military brat and dental hygienist turned serial entrepreneur, Jessica is no stranger to starting over. She took every rock-bottom moment and used it as fuel to rise, healthier, happier, and more successful than ever. Now through her brand Living Unbreakable, she helps women do the same.

Her mission? To help women break free from fear-based beliefs and remember who the hell they are. Expect deep truths, loud laughs, and the kind of tough love that feels like a hug and a slap in the face, at the same time.

Follow me on Instagram @jessica_spence88

MY GIFT TO YOU

I am so glad you're here!

As my Gift to you, get FREE Access to the Living
Unbreakable bonus content by scanning
the QR Code below or visiting
NextStepMortgageGroup.com/book

www.ingramcontent.com/pod-product-compliance
Lightning Source LLC
Chambersburg PA
CBHW021220130626
46554CB00004B/1304